THE KING'S BROADCAST MESSAGE TO THE EMPIRE

OUTBREAK OF HOSTILITIES.

IVYBRIDGE during the Second World War 1939-1945

N.F.S.　　FIRE GUARDS　　P.O.Ws.　　V.E. CELEBRATIONS　　REST CENTRES　　A.R.P.　　SHELTERS

Arthur L. Clamp

Wartime Wedding

This was one of many service personnel weddings which took place in Ivybridge showing the marriage of Sgt. Francis Skelley, R.A., to Priscilla Barnes at St. John's Church, 27th July, 1942. Ken Mitchel is the boy on the left then Mrs. Bessie Barnes, Sgt. Lennard Truscott, Mr. Henry Barnes and Mrs. Clara Skelley and Delsia Barnes make up the wedding group.

This version of the book is virtually as originally published.
There are now additional pages at the back providing informations about the author.

The republishing project is being managed by Arthur's grandson, Steven Gibson. We aim to find all the research that he was involved in publishing, preserving it for the next generation as part of 'The Clamp Collection'.

INTRODUCTION

Fifty years have passed since the ending of this war, familiar faces once seen around are no longer here and many changes have almost obliterated the remains of shelters, etc. once dotted around the town. This illustrated booklet is a part record of those turbulent years when the people of Ivybridge rallied around and responded in a variety ways to the call to arms or to serve on the home front.

It has brought together through photographs, documents and recollections from about forty people a record of the war years which will remind generations to come of the many sacrifices their families made in defending their homeland. It has not been possible to include all the information gathered a much larger publication would be required.

Ivybridge was soon caught up in the war being close to Plymouth which was a prime target for enemy air attacks. War was declared on Sunday, 3rd September, 1939, victory in Europe was declared on 8th May, 1945, and peace finally came with victory over Japan on 14th August, 1945, bringing to a close this conflict with Hitler's armies covering almost six full years.

Plans had been put in hand to set up a civil defence organisation in 1937 which was in a reasonable state of readiness when war was declared. The expected gas attacks did not come but evacuees streamed into the area from London bringing home to local people the first consequences of the war. There was an air of expectedness which was not fulfilled until after the fall of Dunkirk in May, 1940, when enemy forces occupied France. The so called phoney war was over.

The main role that Ivybridge served during the war years was that of an accommodation area for various government departments dislodged from Plymouth through the blitz and the stationing of a variety of naval, army and R.A.F. units here for varying lengths of time. Its country location was considered reasonably safe yet it was only a matter of miles to the coast and Plymouth into which troops moved from this locality in 1944.

In 1940 came the first air attacks; in 1941 came the most serious of them on Plymouth resulting in thousands of people seeking nightly accommodation around the area including Ivybridge. By now the local civil defence organisations were well structured and hundreds of local people threw in their lot in one way or another to support them. There was some ease in 1943 but by now new faces were appearing around the town, U.S. soldiers were here in their hundreds preparing for the Normandy landings in June, 1944.

As the fighting moved across France so the fear of an enemy attack lessened and in its place victory in Europe became increasingly possible. Now more new faces appeared around Ivybridge in the form of Italian and German prisoners of war billeted around the area and made to work on the land until the late 1940s.

Finally happiness and great relief was shown when many of Ivybridge's men and women returned from the battle fronts, from prisoner of war camps, or who were discharged from the forces. The town, like many others, celebrated victory with street parties, dances, bonfires and a host of other events heralding the return to normal life apart, perhaps, from the continuation of rationing.

Acknowledgements and Dedication

A detailed account of this period would simply not be possible without the help of many local people who by loaning photographs and calling on their memories helped to put together this account of the war years. I wish to record my grateful thanks to Walter House, Ivor Martin, Bob Hawton, Peter Wycliffe-Jones, Barbara Morgan, Margaret, Richard and George Pearse, Alec Rogers, John Elford, Noel Blackler, William Bryant, Reginald Vincent, Judy Jago, Sid Short, Don Barwick, Delsia Tremain, Mrs. MacFarlane, Molly Bowden, Joan Dennis and others who gave of their time and patiently searched for answers to my questions.

This title is dedicated to all those who served their country in a thousand ways both at the battle front and on the home front in defence of their country and a way of life enjoyed by generations of Ivybridge people.

Arthur L. Clamp,
203 Elburton Road,
Plymouth, PL9 8HX

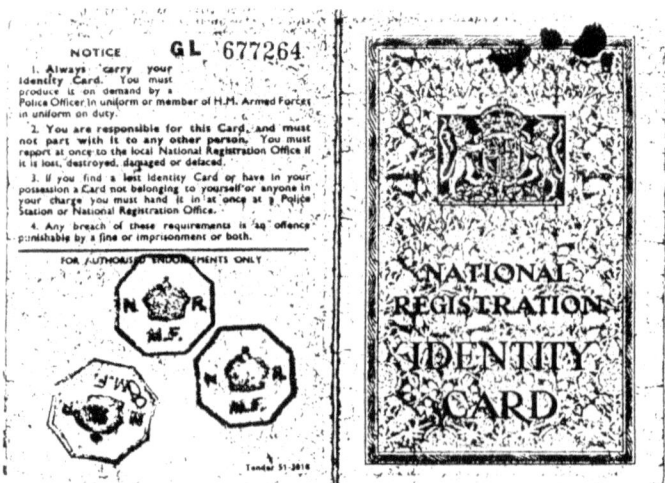

NATIONAL IDENTITY CARDS

This together with the ration book is probably the most well remembered of the various forms used during the war years. Every person had to have one and carry it with them. They were issued from the identity card office at 8 Boringdon Villas, Plympton, run by Sgt. Hill. Police and special constables could demand seeing them and they were necessary for the allocation of ration books from the same address. Introduced in September, 1939, they lasted some years after the war finished.

CIVIL DEFENCE SERVICES

Under the Air Raids Precautions Act, 1937, local ARP organisations were set up throughout the country in anticipation of the outbreak of war. Plymouth was designated a co-ordinated area with Plympton as a sub-control centre under which Ivybridge operated. The lines of communication, training of personnel, etc., came from Plympton as Ivybridge fell in the rural district.

The town's air raid precautions were made up of air raid wardens, a report post in the offices of the mill, two ambulance units, nos. 61 and 62, a first aid post in what was the billiard room of Mr. Harry Wilson's house, Nirvana, Crescent Road, a rescue squad and a decontamination of clothing squad in the event of a gas attack.

The was also the air raid siren operated by those on duty in the mill offices and the fire service with fire guards on duty in or around buildings. Regular training and lectures took place and exercises, usually over a weekend, had to be attended often undertaken with units of the army or with other civil defence units in the R.D.C. area.

These various services functioned throughout the war but were never directly engaged in air raids but the fire service did help out at Plympton and was on stand by during the Plymouth raids.

Due to the enlistment of personnel into the services there was a constant need for replacements with training in first aid and spending some time in the gas chamber at Plympton with a gas mask on for qualification into branches of the civil defence. The headquarters was manned twenty-four hours a day throughout the war by men and women; there were two ARP posts in the mill, one at Lee Mill and another at Harford. These posts were told of coming raids by phone from the mill. The former stables of the mill were fitted out with beds and were used by fire watchers of the mill as was another group in the old tannery building. The apparatus used by the decontamination squad was kept in the mill as was the ambulance used by the two squads, the duties split between both to maintain a twenty-four cover.

Local Reports

Sixty casualties of all descriptions took place in a large ARP exercise in the Ivybridge area on Sunday. Mr. J. Talbot, chief warden for Ivybridge, was in charge of the demonstrations which included damage by HE bombs near *The Sportman's Arms*. The crater formed by the bomb was a dangerous spot and many people were injured. A large number of casualties were found near the electric works where another bomb had fallen. The injured were treated by the First Aid Squads. *February 1940*

An appeal has gone out for more ARP wardens in Ivybridge John Talbot, group warden, reported recently. Volunteers to form decontamination squads are wanted as well. *May 1942*

No. 62 Ivybridge Ambulance Party

Taken in October, 1944, outside the mill's office used as the Head Wardens' post are Mrs. Nelder, William Morris (area training officer), Joan Randall (party leader), Roy Bowden, back row, then Gladys Thorne, Esmé Tebbutt, Mrs. Phillips, Bo Hurrell, Joan Dennis. Front row: Jean Pearse, Molly Fry, Betty Strickland and Joan Thorne.

The Ivybridge A.R.P. Services consist of Air Raid Wardens, Report Post, Ambulance, F.A. Point, Rescue Service, and Decontamination of Clothing. The first four were formed when war became imminent and the remaining two subsequently.

The Ivybridge section being so scattered, it was considered advisable to have four wardens' posts, two in the village, one at Lee Mill and one at Harford, each being manned whenever an "alert" was sounded.

The highest credit is due to the wardens, who have patrolled their sectors during "alerts" in fine weather or foul, by night and day. Another duty of the wardens has been the testing and fitting of respirators on the two occasions the gas van has visited the area to enable residents to have their respirators tested in gas. On each occasion wardens have been in attendance to give advice and to effect any necessary repairs.

1944 report on the Ivybridge Civil Defences.

Ambulance Service

The Ambulance Service has trained constantly and thoroughly —at first under party leaders and subsequently under the area training officer — but, so far, have not been called upon for "active service."

It would not be true, however, to say that they have never had a real casualty with which to deal. During a large scale exercise, in 1941, a soldier was being helped to the waiting casualty car, when the driver, thinking that this was just another mock casualty, said: "You're doing the job properly!" "Properly be blowed!" replied the indignant soldier. "So would you if you'd had a concrete road block dropped on your foot"

Exercises such as this one, and especially the inter-point competitions, arranged by the area training officer, have kept the Ambulance service keen and interested and, incidentally, have made them work hard. The Service has competed in the "Houndiscombe" and "Linda" Cup competitions, taking 3rd place in the former and missing the "Linda" Cup by three points only.

The Point, at which casualties would be cared for pending removal to hospital, situated at "Nirvana," (by permission of Mr. H. Wilson) is in charge of Dr Gregg with a capable team of assistants.

All "Casualtied!"

A number of exercises have been carried out which have included the whole of the services. They have proved most interesting and helpful. At one such exercise the efficacy of tear gas as a harassing agent was fully demonstrated. Tear gas was accidentally released and one of the wardens had an "eye full," and was unable to warn the First Aid Party, proceeding to an "incident," that gas was present, with the result that the whole party became casualties!

Being a part time service, it was to be expected that the personnel would be frequently changed, and it should be borne in mind that much of the credit for the efficiency attained is due to the "pioneers" of the Ivybridge C.D. Services, upon whom fell the work of organisation and initial training. It was during this period that "alerts" were frequent and long, and many hours were spent by night and day, standing by in readiness to respond to calls for help.

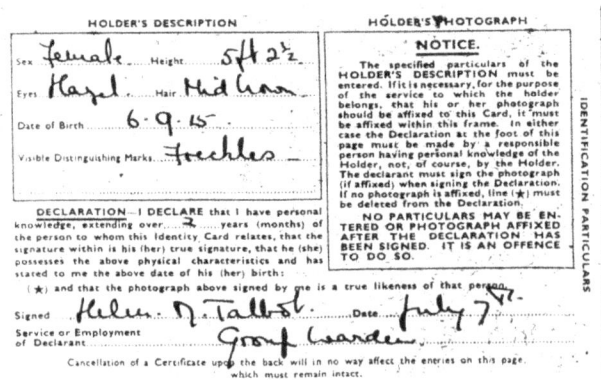

The Rescue Party, formed in May, 1942, under the leadership of "Uncle Sam," have put in 110 training periods and have become proficient in rescuing casualties from bombed houses, across rivers from quarries, etc.

Fine Record

It is a credit to the Party that though they have been in existence such a comparatively short time in a competition with other Rescue Parties in the Plympton area, they gained third place against odds. The weather on the day was foul, and, owing to the luck of the draw they were the last party to compete, so the tackle which they were required to use was wet through and slimy with mud. The members were wet through and would have been much happier at home.

The Decontamination of Clothing Party was the last Service to be formed in Ivybridge. They have been through a course of lectures and training on the decontamination of clothing, using the necessary apparatus installed at Stowford Mills.

Report Post

The Report Post, the manning of which has been, perhaps, the most tedious of all duties, was established at the Stowford Mills offices (by permission of the directors and management). The original siren was the steam siren at the Mill and was sounded by the then Group Warden.

On the Group Warden joining the Forces in July, 1940, the remaining personnel undertook to man the post for 24 hours daily, including week-ends and holidays, and it is to their credit to record that this duty was performed faithfully until Sept. 15th, when the Report Post ceased to function.

See the photograph on the back cover for the C.D. personnel which was taken in 1944.

THE HOME GUARD

On 14th May, 1940, the Secretary of State, the Rt. Hon. Anthony Eden, broadcast an appeal on the radio for volunteers to enlist in local defence units. Within a few days 200,000 men responded by registering at their local police stations. They were known as the *Local Defence Volunteers (LDV)* but Winston Churchill changed their name to the *Home Guard* on 28th July, 1940, which remained until they were stood down in December, 1944. Almost every town or locality had their group of volunteers originally kitted out with an armband and equipped with any firearms they could lay their hands on or even long sticks with metal spikes on the ends.

Ivybridge's Home Guard was No. 12 Platoon with Lt. George A. Mugbridge in charge which was part of the 15th Devon (Plympton) Battalion under Lieut. Col. W. Conran, D.S.O. There was also a mounted company 'B' under a Major W. Ball that was responsible for patrolling on horseback the open moorland as it was thought that enemy parachutists may land on Dartmoor as part of an invasion of this country. This company was one of only two in the whole of the land and involved many men and women who had a good knowledge of the open moor

Although the first volunteers had little equipment and hardly any training their response to night patrols around the town at key points and on the high Beacon was enthusiastically undertaken. The Drill Hall in Victoria Park was their headquarters and on most Sunday mornings there were parades, lectures, demonstrations in the use of equipment, etc. with also an evening parade once a week to which attendance was later made compulsory. There was also a small bore rifle range in the hall. Rifle practice was normally undertaken in the grounds of Cleeve House and from time to time exercises with other platoons took place during weekends involving local civil defence units or with army units stationed in this area and sometimes at Elfordleigh.

Other activities included formation marching around the town usually starting from the Methodist church, taking part in various fund raising parades such as War Weapons Week and, on the lighter side, social events with other home defence units.

By 1941 volunteers had been issued with a uniform and training was being organised in the use of the sten gun, Lewis machine gun, mortars, rifles and the handling of hand grenades and the initial use of the outdated Canadian 300 rifle was discontinued. Ivybridge's platoon had become well organised and was reasonably efficient with training being now undertaken under full time army personnel.

In February, 1942, compulsory enrolment was introduced and the structure of the Home Guard based upon that of the army. The duties of maintaining a vigilant lookout during raids and undertaking guard work and working alongside various forces stationed in the area went on month by month with attendances at week night and weekend parades. Following the successful landings in France in June, 1944, and enemy forces being pushed back across Europe the need for the Home Guard diminished. In December, 1944, the Plympton Battalion which included the Ivybridge Platoon was stood down bringing to an end this local force trained to defend the area had an invasion taken place.

No. 12 Platoon, Ivybridge Home Guard

A group photograph outside of Elfordleigh House, Plympton, probably taken when it was stood down in 1944 shows Major W. G. Ball, holding baton, Lt. George A. Mugbridge, officer in charge of the platoon, then William Hodge, William Northmore, Fred Priddle, Peter Willcocks, John Colwell, Fred Bennett, Jack Turner, Bill Vivian, Freddie Andrews, Arthur Bernard, Ernie Vincent, Frank Lamb, Fred Broom, Clifford Woodley, Clifford Hodge, Jack House, Arthur Johns, Rex Candish, Sid Short, Edward Moysey, ammunition officer, and others.

Cleeve Practice Range

Captain Sparrow loaned his field for weekend rifle practice for the local Home Guard units seen here after the unit was equipped with Canadian rifles in late 1940. Syd Short, Sgt. Ernie Cox, Jimmy Salter, on one knee, Corp. Freddie Andrews, lying down, Bert Foley, Frank Lamb, Tommy Pettifer, Fred Priddle and Fred Broom are recognised here. These meetings usually took place Sunday mornings from 10 a.m. to 12.30 p.m.

L.D.V. Armband

This was the only means of identification for men who made up the Local Defence Volunteers from May to July, 1940.

Lance corporal Tom Pettifer.

Lt. Edward Moysey, 1943

Sgt. Sydney Short, 1943.

Sunday Morning Parade

Six men stand at attention on one of the many weekend parades sometime in 1940. They are Gerald Stoneman, Arthur Northmore, Arthur Johns, Jimmy Salter, Edward Moysey and Frank Davis. They are in Primrose Dairy field and are now equipped with uniforms and guns undergoing training for duty around Ivybridge and for its defence had the enemy landed in this country.

Mounted Ivybridge Cavalary

Dartmoor had to be patrolled and no better way could be had than by horse. Reg German, Admiral Mackworth, George Ryder, Mr. Broom, Bill Greep, Bill Matthews and Harry Hext have been identified in this group on Hangar Down in 1944. They were part of "B" Moorland Company of which undertook night patrols across the open moorland.

AUXILIARY TERRITORIAL FORCES

This was the official title of what was in effect a clandestine network of local groups of men specially trained in guerrilla tactics to operate behind German forces had they landed in England after the fall of Dunkirk in May, 1940. They were unofficially known as Churchill's army and were made up of groups of seven volunteers who had a good knowledge of the local countryside from units of the Home Guard.

Ivybridge had four patrols around its area. There was the Ugborough patrol, Cornwood patrol, Harford patrol and the Flete patrol all under the command of captain Falcon of Slade House, Cornwood. Each patrol had a secret underground bunker which was fitted with beds, lighting and provisioned with food and medical aids. Ugborough's bunker was in Northstock Wood, Cleeve estate, and would have been their operating headquarters.

The volunteers were sworn to secrecy, they had access to a range of explosives and other devices and undertook rigorous training with army personnel in preparation for what would have been a very dangerous task of disrupting enemy forces by blowing up the main railway line, viaducts and any key installations which would be of value to the occupying forces.

There was a Major G. S. Harrison in charge of hundreds of small groups in the county and he was based in Ashburton. The Ugborough patrol was made up of Charles Hine, James Lapthorne, Walter Harper, Anthony Daniels, patrol leader Sgt. Alec Rogers, Maurice Pepperell and Alfred Luscombe. The names are incomplete for the other patrols but remembered is Clifford Andrews, Steve Hoskins, John Andrews, *Cornwood*, Sgt. Baker, Arthur Lloyd, Pedrick, *Flete*, Sgt. F.R. Loveridge, Arthur Perring, H. D. Howell and R. N. Howell, *Harford*.

Alec Rogers recalls that a Lieut. Pearson asked for seven volunteers at a Home Guard rifle practice at Bittaford when these forces were being set up. They met in his barn at Filham a few day later with a Lieut. Roberston who spelt out their intending role had the Germans landed. His barn and lower orchard became the training ground and stores and explosives arrived to be hidden in the barn. They had dynamite, explosive fuses, detonators, hand grenades, time switches, cortex fuse, etc. all necessary for causing as much havoc as possible to the enemy.

Night exercises were often undertaken against other patrols and on one occasion they all met in *The King's Arms*, Ivybridge, to receive medical training in the event of serious injuries and not being able to get access to first aid facilities.

Few people knew of their existence even within families and had the Germans landed the men would have simply disappeared into their bunkers but for how long is questionable in view of the limited food supplies and the might of the enemy forces. However, they kept up their training schedules until the patrols were disbanded in June, 1944, and the bunkers blown up so bringing to an end a branch of the home forces which most people did not know existed.

Churchill's Army at Slade House, Cornwood
This group photograph of the combined local units of the Auxiliary Territorial Forces is thought to have been taken in 1943 during a weekend exercise and briefing activity. The officer in charge, Captain Falcon, lived in the house and the grounds were often used for these meetings away from the public eye.

WARTIME MORTUARY

In anticipation of air raid casualties Ivybridge, like many other towns, had a room set aside referred to as a mortuary. It had three coffins or shells supplied by Plympton R.D.C. made in May, 1941. Fortunately for the town they were not required as the various raids did not give rise to casualties. In June, 1942, an entry in a minute said the chapel (Congregational) and mortuary had a caretaker, Mrs. L. Blight, who was paid £10 a year to keep it in readiness for receiving bodies.

LIGHTING RESTRICTION ORDER 1940

Known as the *Blackout* this order placed severe restrictions on the showing of lights in homes, along streets and main roads, on cars and other vehicles, on bicycles and even carrying a hand held torch. Any light which might draw attention to enemy aircraft flying overhead incurred fines and possibly imprisonment if the offender persisted in flouting this wartime order.

Coupled with this came the painting in white of kerb stones, prominent walls or buildings butting onto a road, the running boards of cars and bumpers, to aid people walking in the dark. Headlamps were shielded with a metal grid to reduce the beam. This was so effective that road accidents resulted in about 9,000 deaths in 1941 the highest on record since they were started in 1928. Even hand held torches had to have two layers of tissue paper over them and the beam should be pointed downwards as the torch was being carried.

A familiar call *Put that light out* was often heard shouted out by wardens patrolling the streets or by special constables who appear to have been less considerate towards people infringing this order. However, people got used to this situation and realised the importance of its adherence. In 1944 the blackout was replaced by the *dim out* when some of the restrictions were lifted and in 1945 all the lighting restrictions were finally lifted.

Removal of Signposts

Also in June, 1940, an order was made for the removal of all road signs, place names, etc. which could indicate to an enemy where he was in this country. Posts were removed, shop boards and village hall notice boards were painted or covered over and any church or business naming the town or village in which it was, in most cases, also covered. However, as the threat of an enemy landing receded this order lapsed in 1943 and signposts, etc. gradually reappeared.

Ringing of Church Bells

June, 1940, also saw the ban on ringing church bells which from this date were only to be rung in the event of an invasion. There were a few exceptions to this order one being they could be rung on Christmas day and Churchill did authorise their ringing to celebrate the success of the El Alamein battle in North Africa.

Immobilising of Vehicles

Owners of any vehicles were ordered to ensure that when their vehicle was left it was to be immobilised by removing its rotor arm from the engine, the ignition key to be taken out and the doors to be securely locked. These precautions were enforced so that any enemy spies or escaped prisoners of war could not gain access to a vehicle. Many people were fined for not complying with this order which was rigidly enforced by the local special constables or police. It came into force in 1940 and was lifted in 1944.

TO BLACKOUT WALKERS

YOUR TURN MAY COME TO-NIGHT

There's danger in the dark. Thousands have already been killed on the roads. Remember — in the blackout the motor driver can't see you until he's almost on top of you. You carry your life on your legs.

WALK **CAREFULLY**

SIGNPOSTS REMOVAL.

INSTRUCTION TO HIGHWAYS AUTHORITIES.

Sir John Reith, Transport Minister, announced in a written Parliamentary reply that highway authorities had been instructed to remove signposts and direction indications which would be of value to the enemy in case of invasion. The work was put in hand on Wednesday.

Some Local Reports

A black out accident occurred at Ivybridge on Saturday evening when Miss B. Bartlet, a nurse from the Mental Hospital, Bittaford, was knocked down by a car. It was driven by F/O F. Kirby of Mount Batten, Plymouth. She has been admitted to the Prince of Wales Hospital, Plymouth. *December 1939*

Failing to comply with the Lighting Restriction Order 1940 for not having bumpers and edges of running boards painted white of his car, Francis R. Brokenshire was fined £1 for each offence. Constable G. E. Webber said that at 7.30 p.m. on 6 February 1941 defendant was having also a defective light. *February 1941*

A driver from Bournemouth was fined £1 for not immobilising his lorry when parked outside of the London Hotel, Ivybridge. A window was left open sufficiently to allow anyone to open the door and no part of the ignition had been removed said PC Reed at Plympton court house. *September 1942*

Mr. W. Hands suggested to the church council that the church should consider the black out of the building, it was decided to act on this matter. *October 1942*

Mrs. O. Pearse, Cadleigh, was cautioned by Constable Richards for driving a motor car, the lights of which did not comply with the Lighting Regulations. *April 1940*

L. Wellington of Ivybridge engineers was fined at Plympton for failing to immobilise a car during the daylight. *August 1940*

A. Kingsland, 25, an Ivybridge mechanic, was fined 10s. at Plympton for using a hand torch not dimmed with two sheets of tissue paper. *December 1940*

W. Sanders, 48, manager of the *Kings Arms* Hotel was fined £2 for failing to obscure a light. *September 1941*

A. R. Whateley, 75, The Recory, Harford, was cautioned by Constable Richards for not having white paint on bumpers and running boards of a car. *December 1942*

RECORD OF RAIDS, BOMBS AND SHELLS FALLING IN THE AREA
as listed in the Plympton Police A.R.P. Book

Ivybridge

27 August 1940:	Langham 3 high explosive bombs, 1 incendiary bomb.
26 August 1940:	Cross Hands Cross 1 AA shell exploded.
21 March 1941:	Field at Hall Farm, Harford 1 high explosive bomb.
23 April 1942:	Field near old toll gate 1 AA shell exploded.
15 February 1943:	Field at Swainstone Farm 1 unexploded AA shell.
16 November 1943:	Pithill Farm AA shell.

Ermington

13 August 1940:	Cadleigh Farm 3 high explosive bombs, damage to Cadleigh Lodge and bungalow.
17 January 1941:	Field at Westlake 2 high explosive bombs.
20 March 1941:	Field at Farms Bridge 2 high explosive bombs. Slight damage to New Park house and shed.
12 August 1943:	Penquit Farm 1 AA shell.
12 August 1943:	Preston Hill 1 unexploded AA shell.
12 August 1943:	Stitson Hill 1 AA shell.

Cornwood

13 August 1940:	Fardell Farm 1 high explosive bomb.
17 September 1940:	Hillson's Brake, Rook Farm 1 high explosive bomb.
17 January 1941:	Quick's clay works 1 AA shell.
13 February 1941:	New Park Wood 1 high explosive bomb.
12 March 1941:	Fields at Broomage Farm 4 high explosive bombs.
20 March 1941:	Near Lee Moor clay pit 1 high explosive bomb.
27 March 1941:	Broomage Wood 1 AA shell.
5 July 1941:	Moorland at Piall's Bridge 300 incendiary bombs.
23 April 1942:	Rook Wood 1 high explosive bomb.
23 April 1942:	New Park waste 2 high explosive bombs.
13 June 1943:	Blatchford 140 incendiary bombs, 1 unexploded bomb.
13 June 1943:	Between Cholwich Town pit and hill 9 phosphorous incendiary bombs damage to Long Row cottages.
13 June 1943:	Cholwich Town 1 high explosive bomb damage to farm windows.
13 June 1943:	Fardell Mill 240 incendiary bombs.
13 June 1943:	Field at Fardell Farm 1 unexploded AA shell.
12 August 1943:	Hanger and Upperton Farms 4 high explosive bombs.
12 August 1943:	Haddown Down, Lutton, 3 high explosive bombs 1 unexploded bomb, 4 phosphorous incendiary bombs.
16 November 1943:	Coombe and Watercombe Farms 13 high explosive bombs 3 unexploded bombs slight damage to nearby house and 2 sheep killed.

Below:
Two diffused incendiary bombs are held by Mr. Ivor Avent recovered by him from his land between Brixton and Ivybridge.

This list has been copied word for word from the police records but from interviews with various people it is incomplete and has spelling mistakes. Although Ivybridge itself was not bombed the surrounding areas were subject to a number of raids and explosive bombs and incendiaries fell from enemy planes on their return from bombing raids up country or from raids on Plymouth. The first bomb dropped in the west country fell near Ivybridge on the lower slopes of the moor but it was the hundreds of incendiary bombs which did some damage to crops and buildings and at Filham injuring a horse at Higher Wellstones farm.

Local Reports
A stirrup pump has been placed in the church vestry, also pails of water and sand in the event of an air raid. *July 1943*
Air raid coded warnings:
Yellow: Early warning
Purple: Imminent
Red: Sound the alarm
Green: Going away
White: All clear
These words could be spoken quickly and were understood by all ARP personnel on duty in the mill offices. They were phoned from Plympton.

AIR RAID SHELTERS

At the outbreak of war Ivybridge was not considered a high risk area and the need for the erection of public shelters was not a high priority. However, like in many other places around Plymouth some local people built their own shelters in gardens or strengthened outbuildings some of which are still standing today.

There were a variety of shelters made and Ivybridge had eventually a few of each placed around the town. There was the Morrison shelter which people could have installed in their homes used as a table providing protection against falling rubble, etc. it being made of a steel frame surrounded with a heavy duty wire mesh. It was named after Herbert Morrison, Minister of Home Security, and half a million were distributed by the end of 1941. Many people slept in them as a matter of course.

The Anderson shelter shown below was erected in gardens and there were some in this area. Again people often slept in them and they have been put to various uses since the war. The much larger public brick built shelters were erected in open areas or along streets and in Ivybridge one was put up where the garage is in Fore Street.

However, with the blitz on Plymouth and the subsequent move from the city of some government departments to Ivybridge priority was given for building three shelters by Stowford Lodge then requisitioned by the Admiralty. One is shown below, the rear of the house was converted into a shelter and an underground one was sited below the south lawn. These were to be used by the Admiralty staff.

Below on the lawn in front of the mill another underground shelter was provisioned with food, etc. set aside for ARP personnel working at their headquarters in the mill offices. There was also another free standing brick shelter here.

Apart from the one public shelter in the Fore Street, private shelters, one for the children of the school, the main concern was for the protection of service and civilian staff working in government offices.

It was the Plympton R.D.C. who was responsible for shelters in the district and they were authorised to go ahead with the construction of hundreds in June, 1940.

Local Reports

After weeks of agitation by Ivybridge parish council the village is to have a surface air raid shelter to hold about 50 people. Plans and tenders for its erection will be shortly put in hand. *September 1940.*

A great need of an air raid shelter for the children of the Council School of Ivybridge was stressed by Mr. J. Freeman at the parish council meeting. He said there were 276 children in the school and that a shelter was essential. The managers had suggested that in the event of a raid the children could take shelter by lying flat alongside the outside wall but this was not satisfactory in wet or cold weather. *October 1940*

Converted Air Raid Shelter

Mr. Walter House is standing besides the bottom section of the shelter erected close to Stowford Lodge which has been used as a small swimming pool.

Anderson Shelter

Named after Sir John Anderson, they were planned in December 1938 and were supplied free of charge to some two and a half million families in the main target areas. They comprised of steel corrugated sheeting lowered into a 4 ft. pit normally dug in a garden then covered over with earth and turf. They gave good protection for six people but were often damp and flooded in times of heavy rain.

PORTALS (JOHN ALLEN & SONS) LTD.
Stowford Mills
Ivybridge
Devon

15th July, 1946

Messrs. Viner, Carew & Co.
Prudential Buildings,
Plymouth.

Dear Sirs,

Re Stowford Lodge, Ivybridge.

As you may have noticed when you called here a month or two ago, to discuss the claim for dilapidations with H.M. Dockyard Representative, there is a large brick Air Raid Shelter on the north side of the house which was put up by the Dockyard.

We shall be glad if you would take up with H.M. Dockyard to have this demolished and carted away.

Yours faithfully,
for PORTALS (JOHN ALLEN & SONS) LTD.

AIR RAID SIREN

If there is any sound that brings back memories of the war it is probably the wailing of an air raid siren. The air raid warning poster gives details of the sounds once familiar to local people.

Use was made at the outbreak of war of the steam siren at the paper mill to warn people of a coming raid. It was sounded by the warden on duty and operated similar to a normal siren except that local people complained they could not always hear it. A new electrical siren was installed as seen in the picture with the boy plugging his ears in July, 1940.

This was in use for the rest of the war replaced later by a normal siren fixed on a tall post on open ground near the *London* inn.

Local Reports

It was stated at a recent meeting of the parish council that several people had complained that they did not hear the air raid siren when it was recently sounded for a practice. *December 1939*

Rumours in Ivybridge that no one will be on duty to sound the siren are without foundation. The duty is being performed as in the past three years by part-time voluntary workers who are on duty all hours of the day and night. *November 1942*

Gas Rattle

This would have been used by a warden in the event of a gas attack as opposed to a siren for an air raid. On its side is stamped "A.R.P., K. Clements and Sons 1939" and Ivybridge would have had three or four to cover the area.

GAS MASKS AND BABY HELMETS

It was anticipated by the government that at the outbreak of war gas attacks would take place throughout the country. Millions of masks were manufactured and distributed with 54,000 given out in the whole of the Plympton rural district which included Ivybridge. People were asked to report to school halls, village and church rooms to be fitted with free gas masks by the local wardens. This was in August, 1939, and in April, 1940, a baby anti-gas helmet had been designed and 700 of these were distributed in the same area.

Everyone was expected to carry their masks with them, however inconvenient it was, and from time to time civil defence exercises were conducted warning civilians that gas would be used. Masks were regularly tested especially for children at schools and local reports tell of mobile gas testing vans going around the area undertaking this by the wardens. However, by the middle of 1942 the threat of a gas attack had receded and from about this time masks were not generally carried apart from the wardens, special constables and others on duty.

It is recorded that 2,000 gas masks were issued in Ivybridge and that on at least two occasions a gas testing van came from Plympton in May, 1941, and July, 1942, testing and modifying masks mainly for school children. This was undertaken by the air raid wardens.

Two Local Reports

W. Hart, aged 18, volunteer in the Home Guard, reported that his service respirator was stolen in the Masonic Hall. *February 1942*

When it was announced by the clerk that a van to test gas masks was visiting Ivybridge on 20th July, 1942, several councillors spoke how vital it was for the public to avail themselves of this opportunity. The van is to be placed in Victoria Park. It was resolved to ask the School Managers to get the children to have their respirators attended. *July 1942*

Wearing Gas Masks at Play

Jill, Noel and Ian Blackler were encouraged by their mother to practise wearing a mask as seen here in their garden at 14 Fore Street, Ivybridge, riding on their scooters.

Fitting Gas Masks

It was normally the A.R.P. who issued gas masks to children and adults and checked that they fitted properly as seen here in this Plymouth photograph. This kind of scene would be typical of many areas including Ivybridge as masks were also checked from time to time. A Mrs. Lowry is remembered as helping in this work in Ivybridge.

FOOD, CLOTHING AND FUEL RATIONING

Although it may have not been realised at the outbreak of war that rationing at a local level would soon take place the very heavy shipping losses sustained by the Allies when bringing in food and other supplies quickly dispelled this view.

Rationing was introduced in January, 1940, although the Ministry of Food had been set up in 1937 in anticipation of this country going to war with Germany. Food was stored in very large depots and the country was divided into regions for its distribution. Millions of ration books were printed and people had to obtain one in order to buy food. There was also a clothing book issued and a Motor Fuel ration book for persons with authorised vehicle use.

Everyone had to register with a butcher, grocer and milkman and remained with them unless they moved away. Coupons were handed in for food and clothing in addition to money and this system enabled a strict control to be exercised over the consumption of food and use of other items.

It must, however, be said that there was in most areas a flourishing black market in food, etc. and extra amounts could sometimes be obtained by paying more than the market price or by knowing where unregistered supplies were available.

The average housewife had to exercise great skill and, many times, patience and good judgement when using up the family weekly coupons. National newspaper advertisements gave advice on a balanced food programme; allowances changed from time to time and rationing was not fully lifted until as late as 1954.

The weekly ration in May, 1941, was: 3 pints of milk, 9 ozs of jam, 7 ozs of butter; ½lb of sugar, 2 ozs of tea. 1/- worth of meat (rationed by price), 4 ozs of bacon, 1½ ozs of cheese and 2 ozs of cooking fat.

People did not have to register with one shop for clothing but it was still a problem to cloth the family adequately and very often ladies used their sewing skills in making garments or converting blankets into coats, etc.

The allowance in 1941 was: shirt 5 coupons, main jacket 13 coupons, tie 1 coupon and so on. Each person had 66 coupons for a year, later reduced to 48, and utility clothes and furniture was introduced in 1942.

Food Control Office

The implementation of the rationing scheme for this area was undertaken from Boringdon Villas, Plympton, by Captain A. Langbourne with a staff of about ten and a further ten staff when ration and clothing books were given out in all the villages in the rural district area including Ivybridge. The Methodist church hall was used on occasions.

Some 22,000 books were given out each year by teams working from the Plympton office using schools, village and church halls where people had to collect their books. There was also a Milk Office at Boringdon Villas which dispensed dried milk, concentrated orange juice and cod liver oil for children. Special coupons were issued and this supplementary food was free

Local Reports

S. Hoskin, aged 48, of Venton Farm, farmer, was summoned 10s. for killing two pigeons under the Defence Regulations, 1939. *June 1940*

Albert Mattacott, butcher, Fore Street, Ivybridge, was fined £14 for selling meat in excess of maximum allowed (rationing order). *October 1940*

W. R. West, *Smith's Arms*, Lee Mill, was fined £2 for unlawfully accepting 5 gallons worth of petrol coupons contrary to the Motor Fuel Rationing Order, 1941. *June 1941*

W. Fry, Western Road, Ivybridge, was fined 10s. for the illegal use of petrol in a motor car. *April 1943*

Timetable of Rationing

Tea	1940 to 1952
Sugar	1940 to 1953
Cream	1940 to 1953
Butter	1940 to 1954
Meat	1940 to 1954
Petrol	1940 to 1950
Shell eggs	1941 to 1953
Cheese	1941 to 1954
Clothes	1941 to 1949
Jam	1941 to 1948
Sweets	1942 to 1953
Bread	1946 to 1948

Pool Petrol

This was the only grade of petrol available and in December, 1939, it was increased in price by ½d. bringing it to 1s. 10d. a gallon the highest since February, 1924, when it was 1s. 11d. a gallon.

Picking Rose Hips

Adults and children were encouraged to pick rose hips for which they were paid 2d. a pound. The W.V.S. organised this and set a target for the Plympton R.D.C. of 2 cwt. in October, 1943. The hips were a source of vitamin C and were made into rose hip syrup. Pickers had to note that hips had to be picked dry, be a nice red colour and have no stalks.

DEVON COUNTY HERB COMMITTEE

60 Tons of Hips urgently needed from Devon.

The Children's supply of Vitamin C.

PICK THE HIPS WHEN DRY AND JUST TURNING RED.

Please take the Hips to any of the following Collecting Centres which have been recognised by the Devon County Herb Committee.

2/- for 14 lbs. paid for freshly gathered Hips.

COLLECTING CENTRES:

Dartmouth :	Mr. Horrell, Market Street, Dartmouth. (Monday Afternoons.)
Ivybridge :	Mrs. Talbot, Gerston, Ivybridge.
Kingsbridge :	Mrs. Thomas, W.V.S., Fore Street, Kingsbridge.
Plympton :	W.V.S., 8, Bodington Villas, Plympton.

Food Dumps and Voluntary Food Organisers

In 1940 following the evacuation of Allied Forces from Dunkirk, France, it was thought that an invasion of England would take place by German troops (Hitler had planned to launch *Sea Lion*, an assault from France in September, 1940, but turned his troops eastwards to open up the Russian front).

Voluntary food organisers were appointed throughout the Plympton Rural District. W. G. Hands, of Ivybridge, represented this area on an eight-man committee which was set up in September, 1940. They were responsible for the handling of emergency food supplies, to advise householders to stock flour and at least one week's unrationed foodstuffs. They were also to organise the distribution of food reserves under seven commodities.

Food dumps were established throughout the rural district and were maintained until 1945 when a local report referred to them being removed.

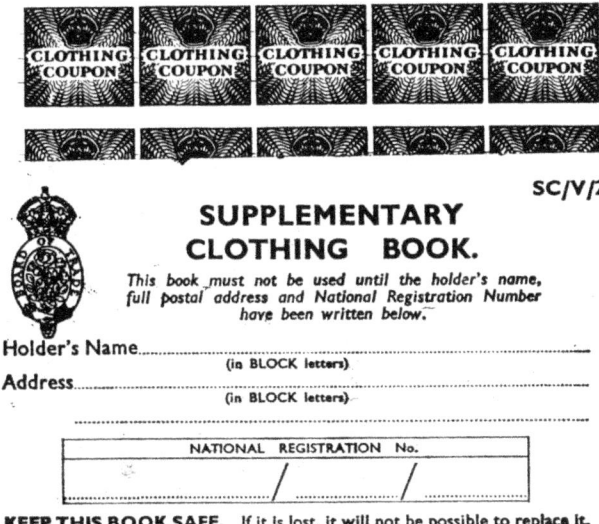

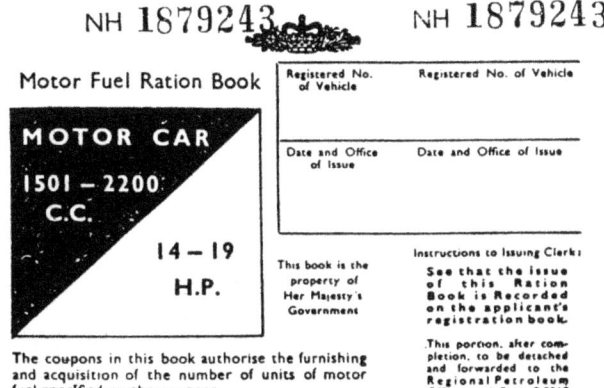

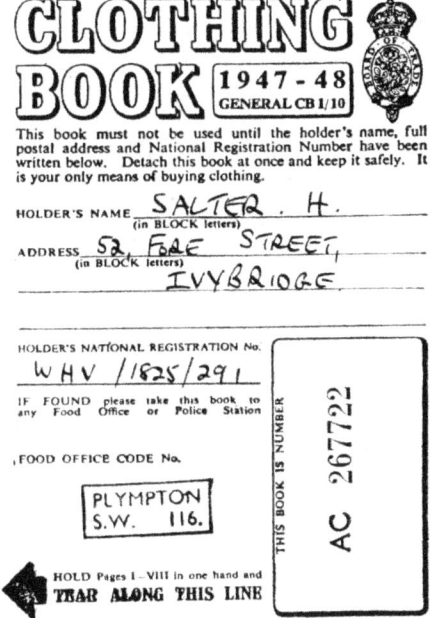

Wartime Rationing

A familiar sight still for many people are these four examples of the many books, certificates and coupons required to buy food, petrol and clothing.

THE FIRE SERVICES

Ivybridge's involvement in this area was three fold. It had its own Auxiliary Fire Service with the fire station in Western Road, there were fire guards or watchers which did duty at the paper mill and Lee's Mill and there was the National Fire Service No. 7 Regional Training Establishment at Lee Mill where about 2,800 men and women undertook a variety of training courses in fire fighting before entering the various fire services in the West Country.

The A.F.S. was set up under the Air Raid Precaution Act, 1937, to ensure that every town had some means of fire fighting capacity in the event of air raids. Volunteers were called for to undertake training and fire duties throughout the war years. Ivybridge's fire service was well under way by 1940 equipped with a Leyland fire engine, a new station built in Western Road, an average of twelve men who maintained a round the clock duty by being available for immediate call out from their work, attending weekly practices and lectures and participating in various civil defence exercises and events in the area. There was also a women's section at Ivybridge.

In August, 1941, the network of local stations came together as the National Fire Service (N.F.S.) by which fire appliances could be moved from area to area in the event of a major blitz which soon occurred on Plymouth. The local stations were equipped by the Home Office and personnel trained by full time firemen resulting in quite a high standard of response. There was a station leading fireman, leading firemen and firewomen. The N.F.S. was stood down in March, 1945, with many local stations closing but not including Ivybridge's which continued as part of No. 19 area Fire Force.

The fireguards were all local volunteers who did duty either in certain buildings or areas during the nights and were trained to deal with the large number of incendiary bombs which fell on towns quickly setting alight buildings, etc. but for Ivybridge this was not fortunately a great danger. As men were frequently called up for war service compulsory fire watching duties were introduced in 1942 with training and attendance at lectures.

The largest presence of fire personnel was at Lee Mill where a training camp was set up when the N.F.S. came into being in 1941 lasting throughout the war. It was equipped with drill towers, fire engines, staff and hutted accommodation for trainees on its various courses. Canadian firemen who had come over to help in Plymouth also trained at Lee Mill.

Local Reports

Mr. W. Hands of Cleeve House, Ivybridge, who recently retired from the special constabulary has now been appointed senior Fire Guard for this area. *August 1942*

An N.F.S. Fordson lorry driven by Fireman L. A. Woodroffe, aged 32, of No. 7 column, Lee Mill Camp, collided with a U.S. Army towing truck on the road to Plympton. *August 1944*

Over 100 fire guards attended a lecture and demonstration in the playground of the council school on Tuesday. Mr. Hands, chief fire guard, introduced captain Hosking of Plympton who gave the lecture on fire procedures. *October 1944*

Ivybridge N.F.S. towing vehicle crashed on Monday evening while going to Plympton for a practice. The top part of the van hit an electric light standard at Woodlands Corner. Four part-time firemen were hurt, Alan Shepherd, Cyril William, John William and Alan West. After treatment by Dr. W. Trumper of Ivybridge they proceeded home. *October 1944*

National Fire Service, No. 7 Regional Training Establishment, Lee Mill. Senior company officer is J. D. Chadwick. *October 1944*

An appeal has gone out for volunteers to man the pumps was made by Comp. Officer E. Northcott and Section Leader R. Pedrick. The pump will be withdrawn if men do not come forward. *May 1945*

Trained Firemen at Lee Mill

Another group of firemen pose for the photographer after completing a training course at No. 7 Regional Training Establishment. No date has been given but the column officer and two training instructors are in the middle row. A drill tower stands behind and part of an auxiliary towing vehicle can be seen.

SPECIAL CONSTABLES and POLICE

Many local men were appointed special constables under the War Emergency Regulations to assist the full time police and to undertake on a roster basis duties such as the enforcement of the blackout, checking identity cards and ensuring that people complied with changing regulations.

Forty-seven men were sworn in in 1938 with a further twenty-three during the war years to cover two beats, Ivybridge and Harford, with parts of Ermington, Cornwood and Plympton. They had special training and were a familiar sight patrolling each locality especially when called out during raids. They had an unenviable task of enforcing restrictions and were often open to abuse.

The full-time police serving at the station were:
Constable W.H. Cockram, 1930-1942
"   W. Richardson, Lee Mill, 1935-1941
"   G. Baverstock, 1931-1952
"   A. Reed, 1937-1943

Their duties were very demanding during the war years reporting the movement of aliens, recording incidents between troops and civilians often actually sorting out troubles themselves, ensuring the orderly distribution of ration books together with reporting of raids, plane crashes, escaped or injured prisoners, etc.

Ivybridge Special Constables, June 1943
Back row: M. P. Snell, E. O. Damerell, H. W. Blight, A. Fare, F. R. Hawton, H. Hancock, A. L. Guey.
Middle row: W. Varcoe, E. G. Curson, A. L. Clarke, W. Pippin, S. E. Varcoe, G. T. Sandover, G. Marshall.
Front row: E. Hancock, A. C. Browne, R. Stephen, F. Baker, W. E. Fry, W. T. Withycombe. Area officer F. H. Passy, Group Sergeant A. P. Abbott.

Digging for Victory
Four boys are at work at Bridge Park making their contribution for the war effort. The changing room and wire netting of the tennis club can be seen in the background.

EVACUEES COME TO DEVON

At the outbreak of war in September, 1939, thousands of children and mothers with babies were evacuated from London to various areas of the country including Devon.

One train out of hundreds which left the capital carried 700 children and teachers from Acton Wells School and Acton Technical School leaving Paddington at 10.30 a.m. and arriving at Plymouth at 4 p.m. on 1st September. The detraining officer was Major Helston, water and light refreshments were handed out to the tired children and twenty buses were lined up to take them to different parts of south Devon with 150 to Ivybridge, 100 to Ermington, 100 to Cornwood and others further afield. They were grouped in tens with an adult or teacher.

Upon arrival at Ivybridge they assembled in the council school and under the guidance of the billeting officer local people either volunteered to take as many as they could or, in some cases, the children were allocated to homes where rooms were known to be unused. So Ivybridge had its first encounter of war with this influx of young peoople filling its school and making all kinds of demands upon the village.

The anticipated heavy bombing of London at the outbreak of hostilities did not take place and many of the children returned to London within six months the largest group leaving for Buckinghamshire in November, 1939, when boys from the technical school were taken by train from Ivybridge station to continue their training closer to London.

It appears that the majority of London children settled into their new homes without too much difficulty but no doubt tears were shed, sleepless nights experienced and even the kindness of Ivybridge people could not be an adequate substitute for their own homes. It must also be said that some childrens' manners and ways caused consternation at first and local reports speak of children having lice, not liking local food, their language and words were somewhat different from Devon's but these differences soon merged with local ways. Parents came down from time to time to visit their children and, in a few instances, became evacuees themselves moving away from London when the bombing started in 1940-41.

There were throughout the war other evacuees who made their way to Devon but not on the scale of the 1939 exodus. For Ivybridge most of these had left by 1942 by which time troops were being drafted into the area for quite different reasons.

Two German Jewish refugee boys who left their country earlier this year were among the Acton evacuees at Ivybridge. *September 1939*

The Acton boys who have been billeted at Ivybridge since the beginning of the war are leaving for Wolverton, Buckinghamshire. The Penzance Paddington train will stop especially at Ivybridge at 8.30 a.m. and will include three coaches for the boys. Their luggage is being sent on today in a special luggage van. The boys are entering the Technical College at Wolvercote. *9 November 1939*

Mrs. A. Woolner of Acton, London, complained through the Area Billeting officer that 9s. had not been refunded to her by the person billeting her son Dixon. *February 1940*

An appeal was made by Mrs. H. Jenkins of Lee Moor requesting that the boy now billeted with her be removed on the grounds that he was dirty in his habits. *March 1940*

Leonard Shephard, 13 years, and Philip Ottley, 13 years, school boys evacuated from London to Brixham were found asleep in a telephone kiosk at Wrangaton at 11.15 p.m. They had two pedal cycles stolen from the rear of a cinema in Paignton. *November 1940*

These boys of Acton Technical College left Ivybridge in November, 1939, to continue their technical education in Buckinghamshire.

OUTLINE OF GOVERNMENT SCHEME

The arrangements which are being made provide for dispersal from the crowded towns where the results of air attack would be most serious. In this movement priority will be given to children, and school children will, as far as possible, be moved school by school, accompanied by their teachers and other helpers. Where this arrangement is made householders will be asked to board and lodge the children. Homes are to be found for them in the districts to which they are to be taken: that is why arrangements must be planned in advance. Householders who provide such homes will be paid by the Government at the rate of 10s. 6d. a week where one child is taken and 8s. 6d. a week for each child where more than one child is taken.

Children under school age will be accompanied by their mothers or some other person who will be responsible for looking after them. In these cases the householder will only be asked to provide lodging, not board, and payment will be made at the rate of 5s. a week for each adult and 3s. a week for each child. Payment at the rate of 5s. a week will be made by the Government where the householder provides lodging for a teacher or helper accompanying a party of school children.

Arrangements for the necessary transport and for increased supplies of food to be made available for shopkeepers will be made by the Government.

Equipped with gas masks London children leave for the west country in September 1939.

Evacuation Stops.

NO MORE UNACCOMPANIED LONDON CHILDREN.

The Government has decided to suspend after November 10th the organised evacuation of unaccompanied children from London, states the Ministry of Health.

During the last twelve months parties of school children have left London at fortnightly intervals, but recently the response has been very small.

The Government considers that at the present juncture the periodical evacuation of small parties of unaccompanied children is not warranted.

5.11.42

A St. John's Ambulance nurse is handing out drinks to London evacuees at Plymouth railway station. *September 1939*

Evacuees knitting for the troops while sitting on the steps of Ivybridge school. *September 1940*

Leaving Ivybridge

Boys of Acton Technical School who were evacuated to Ivybridge at the beginning of the war are now about to leave for Buckinghamshire. They are seen here enjoying a last walk around Ivybridge before departing. *November 1939*

REFUGEES FROM PLYMOUTH'S BLITZ AND REST CENTRES

The extensive raids on Plymouth not only caused severe disruption of city life but imposed an almost intolerable burden on surrounding towns and villages through thousands of people trekking out each evening to avoid the night raids. At the height of this almost daily exodus something like 50,000 people made for the relative safety of the countryside during the most severe raids in March, 1941.

The rural district of Plympton, which took in Ivybridge was inundated with people coming on foot, bicycle, car and in any other form of transport resulting in about 7,000 people sleeping in any building or vehicle. Almost every building was occupied including schools, church halls, village halls, churches and homes offering some kind of accommodation for the night. People also slept in cars, corporation buses, barns and even alongside hedges such was the fear of remaining in Plymouth during a night's raid.

Thirty-seven rest centres had been opened in the rural district by March, 1941, many as huts specially put up for this purpose. Mr. Owen Johns, superintendant of Plympton hospital, was in overall charge going around night by night ensuring an adequate supply of food and bedding. Mr. Hands was responsible for the Ivybridge rest centres as listed below in the August, 1941, report.

Many families opened up their homes to relatives and friends living in Plymouth and an official report said that the council school rest centre quickly filled up each evening, lorries arrived in Ivybridge loaded with people, buses filled to capacity quickly unloaded their passengers and returned to Plymouth. The Methodist church hall served tea and refreshments to the trekkers and on occasions over a thousand people arrived in the village with 300 sleeping in its cinema. On 21st April, 1941, twenty to thirty cars were parked along the Ivybridge road with their owners and families asleep in them.

The W.V.S., church groups, individuals and families rallied to the plight of the trekkers supplying refreshments, helping with the bedding, providing food in the morning and helping in many other ways. A mobile canteen made a regular appearance at the centres offering refreshments run by the W.V.S.

So Ivybridge like many other places near Plymouth did its part in helping those caught up in the blitz giving support where needed and providing accommodation often at very short notice.

Local Reports

Plymouth people who sleep in the Ivybridge rest centres were told on Monday by the billeting officer that the centre will be closing after Tuesday night. Each night hundreds of Plymothians make their way here with their families with blankets, food and clothing in bags, carriers and cases to spend the night. Many also sought accommodation in private houses but had to return to Ivybridge where the billeting officer had to open Ivybridge Council School for the night. *June 1941*

Mr. W. Hands stated that he had opened the church room for the people from the blitz of Plymouth. *July 1941*

Provision at Ivybridge for rest centres is: Council School, 220 sleeping, 108 meals, contact Mr. Seddon. Also at Belle Vue, Exeter Road, Methodist and Congregation school rooms, parish church hall and the Erme Masonic Lodge. *August 1941*

A canteen was installed in the Rest Centre at Ivybridge Council School. *April 1943*

People leaving Plymouth by lorry

The Evening Trek Out

List of Country Rest Centres in the Plympton Relieving Officer's Area indicating the number of people sheltering on 24 April 1941 compared with the normal scheduled accommodation

Rest centre		Schedule	Numbers on 24/4/41
Plympton	Grammar School	300	750
	Senior School	400	1000
	St Mary's School	200	678 (with church)
	Institution	–	40
	Underwood Mission	–	110
	St Maurice Guildhall	150	300
	Church Room	–	300
	Salvation Army and Recreation Hut	–	200
	Colebrook Mission	–	90
	Ridgeway	–	350
Ivybridge	School and Hall	500	1000
Lee Mill	Chapel	60	110
Shaugh			94
Sparkwell		100	120
Cornwood		50	140
Ermington		–	40
Yealmpton	School	150	200
	Hall	–	180
Plymstock	School	150	250

The actual numbers of refugees are given here for 24th April, 1941, at the height of Plymouth blitz, showing Ivybridge, Lee Mill, Cornwood and Ermington numbers.

WOMENS VOLUNTARY SERVICE

This was founded by Lady Reading in 1938; its members were not paid, there was no system of ranks yet by the 1940s a million ladies had joined. It became well known for providing cups of tea in a crisis bit its role was much greater providing food, shelter, information, staffing rest centres, incident posts, working field kitchens, "dust bin ovens", ran mobile canteens, clothing depots, made camouflage netting, collected salvage and books among other duties.

Many ladies spent countless hours undertaking a variety of jobs in Ivybridge, some of the duties could be done in their homes, others in halls, the school or staging demonstrations of emergency cooking, etc. Uniforms were provided for many of the volunteers when on duty especially during the raids. Although there was no special building designated as a WVS office in Ivybridge the work undertaken here was done thoroughly and with a good heart.

Ivybridge W.V.S. have arranged a demonstration of emergency cooking to be given in one of the huts in the Park at 3 p.m. Anyone interested is welcome to attend. W.V.S. members give valuable help to the Dame Hannah Rogers Orthopaedic Hospital twice a week washing and ironing children's clothing. Mrs. Talbot at Gerston would welcome more support.

Ivybridge Camouflage Netting Group

W.V.S. members and families are recorded here working at the school in October, 1942. Recognised are Dorothy Bastard, Helen Talbot, Bessie Barnes, Mrs. Vincent, Mrs. B. Winston, Roy Priddle, John Talbot, Jim Hucker, Doreen Vincent and Mrs Jemit among other.

Basic Training for all W.V.S. Members.

The following is an extract from a letter received from the Dowager Marchioness of Reading, D.B.E., Chairman of W.V.S.—

" To all W.V.S. members—We have all heard and thought much during the past few months about total war, and the need for more effort, more sacrifice, and more precaution for any trial which Total War may bring us. I feel we must now consider not only as individuals, but also as a service, what further contributions we can make to the war effort.

Our full title is Women's Voluntary Services for Civil Defence, and however many different types of work we may undertake we must remember that our first duty is Civil Defence. This becomes increasingly important as the regular Civil Defence personnel is depleted by other war demands and our aim should be to form a second line.

In order to achieve this I am asking every member of W.V.S. to take a short course of training in Civil Defence; this will consist of five talks on Immediate Aid, Anti-Gas, Fire Fighting, Elementary A.R.P., and the place of W.V.S. in Civil Defence, but I hope many members will go on to take a more complete training.

Mrs Mabel Algar at Filham House
wearing her W.V.S. uniform

WOMENS LAND ARMY

This was formed in June, 1939, by Lady Denman, D.B.E., who was its director for most of the war years. With the prospect of thousands of men enlisting into the services who were working on the land the government backed this scheme to train women to take their places. County offices were set up and in Devon there were 114 recruits in 1939 rising to 1,071 by 1943 falling to 360 when the W.L.A. was disbanded in 1950. There were 80,000 members at its height in 1946.

The weekly pay was £1 8s. for 54 hours of work, accommodation was often in hostels, such as the one at Lyneham House, or in homes or farms. A uniform was supplied and members could be moved around where work was required to be done. The women undertook a wide range of work from harvesting, hoeing, milking, mucking out, etc. according to the season of the year. Farmers would let the gang leader at Lyneham House know how many extra hands they could do with and lists would be read out most mornings telling the girls where they were going to work. A lorry took them in the morning and collected them late afternoon. They could easily be working in a variety of places over the months apart from those living in with farmers who normally worked on one farm.

The sight of the girls being taken around each day and working on the land was a familiar one and at times they would join local men and troops at dances. Miss Rosemary Martin of Lee Moor House was in overall charge of the Ivybridge area. Mr. Alec Rogers at Filham recalls the WLA helping out pulling kale, Mr. S. Pearse, Coyton Farm, had Joyce Rich living in with others girls coming to help occasionally. Mr. Bert Endacott, Fore Street, had help in delivering milk with an army girl. Mr. F. Leveridge has Miss G.M. Grainger living in at Lukesland Farm helping with the poultry units. Perhaps the longest serving member was Joy Cane who lived in for four and a half years at Dinnaton Farm worked then by Mr. Willcocks. There were many more around Ivybridge.

Local Reports

W.L.A. Work. Rats are having a bad time in the Ivybridge district just now. The cause is none other than two charming young women, one an American from Illinois and the other from Leeds. Trained in north Devon they are sent and paid by the Devon War Agricultural Committee and are provided with bicycles to go from place to place using gas or poison bait. *October 1942*

More than 30 W.L. Army girls live at Lyneham House and worked like trojans in the district. Most of them are helping with the harvest but also do hoeing and market gardening. They have a gramophone in the hostel but want more records and they have a pianist but no piano. *September 1943*

Armband and recruiting poster.

On the way to Work

Although this photograph is not in the Ivybridge area it will remind many people of this familiar sight when girls were taken and returned each day to their hostel at Lyneham House. It is a Devon War Agricultural Committee lorry on His Majesty's Service. The year is 1944.

UNIFORM

On joining the W.L.A. every girl is supplied with the following: 2 green jerseys, 2 pairs of breeches, 2 overall coats, 2 pairs of dungarees, 6 pairs of stockings, 3 shirts, 1 pair of ankle boots, 1 pair of shoes, 1 pair of gumboots or boots with leggings, 1 hat, 1 overcoat with shoulder titles, 1 oilskin or mackintosh, 2 towels, an oilskin sou'-wester, a green armlet, and a metal badge. After every six months of satisfactory service she receives a half-diamond to be sewn on the armlet; she has a special armlet after two years' service, and a scarlet armlet to replace the two-year one after four years' service.

Every twelve months she is entitled to some uniform replacement. All uniform is of course given free of charge, though she has to surrender a certain number of coupons.

2072 FLIGHT AIR TRAINING CORPS

Ivybridge's A.T.C. was well supported throughout the war under the leadership of Pilot Officer A. H. Thorne, its headquarters being at Factory Bridge in the former Salvation Army hut. It was formed in February, 1941, with twenty-three boys prior to which the Ivybridge lads had to go to South Brent where there was a flight already in existence.

The aim of the corps was to train young boys in aircraft recognition, navigation, drill, etc. in preparation for their likely enlistment into the R.A.F. A week's training at an airfield in Somerset would also give an opportunity for them to experience flying alongside experienced crews. The photographs and articles on theses two pages record much of 2072 Flight. Dozens of Ivybridge boys joined, many being called up for service but their place soon being taken by new recruits. The turnover in the corps was high and these three photographs record just a few of the many boys who served in this flight.

On August Bank Holiday a shoot took place at Lee Mill with cadets A. Lake, G. Priddle, P. Barker, R. Clarke, Sgt. Brown, D. Mackay, K. Thorne, K. Short, S. Bastard and S. Newcombe. *1942*

Sgt. Pilot Frank Prout, 19 year old son of Mr. and Mrs. J. P. Prout, Ivybridge, is spending his leave helping with the training of his old Flight (No. 2072 Ivybridge-Brent). He joined the A.T.C. when it was formed at South Brent. Another Ivybridge boy is Sgt. Pilot R. Bush who has gone to Coastal Command. The Flight now has over 40 members. *April 1943*

Six boys of the Ivybridge-Brent Flight A.T.C. will be joining the R.A.F. for service as air crew and other duties. They are Sgt. B. Gordon, Sgt. K. Short, Cpl. G. Priddle, Cpl. A. Prowse, Cadet C. Hawkins and Cadet G. Phillips. *October 1943*

There is an R.A.F. exhibition in Ivybridge this week where the Air Training Corps are recruiting. In the window of Mr. Backhouse's wireless shop in the main street there is a display of model aircraft, a bomb sighting and training equipment. Recruits can obtain booklets about the A.T.C. from the shop or council school. *January 1944*

Ivybridge section of 2072 Flight will parade as part of the 3rd birthday of the foundation of the Air Training Corps. There will be a march past and service at St. John's Church, Ivybridge, of its thirty-two members. P/O A. H. Thorne o/c started the section with twenty-three members. *February 1944*

H.Q. FOR A.T.C. AT IVYBRIDGE

Hut May be Opened Shortly

The Salvation Army has notified Ivybridge A.T.C. of its willingness for them to use a hut in the village as a recreational and training centre, and negotiations are taking place regarding the renovation of the premises. There is a possibility of its opening in a few weeks' time after the premises have been reconditioned and lighting installed.

A generous donation to the funds has been forwarded by a local officer, Lieut. L. Watkins, R.N.V.R., who, in an accompanying letter, writes: "Although not in the Royal Air Force, I have a very high opinion indeed of the Air Training Corps."

A brother of Lieut. Watkins is very likely to supply an I.C. engine for installation in the hut, for the cadets to strip and reassemble.

It is hoped, also, to purchase equipment for throwing enlarged pictures and silhouettes of planes on to a screen.

Funds Rolling In

Mrs. Lowrey's second whist effort for the Fund (which is nearing £30) realized £1 17s. 6d. This time it was a tournament, at the Masonic Hall last Saturday, with the following results:—

First lady and gent.—Mrs. Booth and Mrs. Bowden.

Second lady and gent.—Mrs. Fremantle and Mrs. Gall.

Parades

To-night (Friday).—19.00, Flight Drill; 19.30, Aircraft Recognition Test, conducted by Mr. Farley (Royal Observer Corps, Plympton), at the Council School.

Tuesday, Sept. 29.—19.00, Concert Rehearsal; at the Schoolroom.

Wednesday, Sept. 30. — 19.00, Flight Drill; 19.30, First-Aid; 20.30, Morse; at the Schoolroom.

October 1942

A TON OF BOOKS

Ivybridge Effort to Help A.T.C. Flight

Ivybridge householders will have an opportunity of helping both the war effort and the local flight of the Air Training Corps.

Next week a special house-to-house collection of books, magazines and papers will be made by members of the A.T.C. on Wednesday and Saturday afternoon.

Proceeds will go to the fund to provide the flight with a suitable headquarters and a recreational fund, premises for which have already been acquired.

On Monday afternoon a loudspeaker van, which will be operated by Mr. Douglas, the local represntative of the Waste Paper Recovery Association, accompanied by cadets, will parade the district to remind people that the collection is being made.

As no special effort has taken place previously, it is hoped that at least a ton of books, etc., will be collected.

September 1942

Roy Abbott and Ivor Willis are the two cadets in the April, 1945, picture.

AIR Training Corps cadets of Lee Mill congratulate their sergeant, N. A. J. Abbott, upon his promotion to flight-sergeant and being selected to represent his squadron at an A.T.C. national rally in London, from May 11 to 14, when he will be a guest at among other entertainments, the England v. Scotland match at Tottenham Football Ground; A.T.C. boxing championships at the Royal Albert Hall; a film, "Henry V." at the Stoll Theatre; and a sightseeing tour of London.

On Sunday, May 13, there is to be a march past in Hyde Park, at which the salute will be taken by Marshal of the Royal Air Force Sir Charles Portal, G.C.B., D.S.O., M.C.

More Names

Recognised here are Norman Abbott, Maurice Willcocks, Walter House, Ken Penwill, Ken Thorne, Dereck Carline with P/O Alf Thorne and Allen Lake.

Within twelve hours of his arrival home in this country from Canada, where he has graduated as a navigator and bomb-aimer, Sergt. Jack Lobb, R.A.F., of Bittaford, was back with his former colleagues of Ivybridge Section, A.T.C., giving instruction. All the cadets in the navigation class with whom he is shown above, were in the Flight when Sergt. Lobb joined the Royal Air Force, in March, 1943.

Ivybridge Air Training Corps

Mr. C. Lee, Mr. A. Ward, Mr. G. Lee, K. Short, G. Priddle, T. Broome, G. Phillips, J. Chapman, R. Leach, C. Hawkins, P. Barter, G. Gordon, K. Thorne, H. Hall, A. Lake P.O., A. H. Thorne, officer in charge, W. Wilcoy, D. Carline, A. Prowse, K. Penwell, N. Abbott, W. House, K. Broome, D. Barnes.

Girls Training Corps

The local newspaper article records the formation of an Ivybridge section at the beginning of February, 1943, when thirty girls enrolled at its first meeting in the council school. In March, 1943, a brief report stated that thirty girls received their enrolment badges from Miss Maybee, county organiser, in the Methodist school room.

By June, 1943, its commandant was Miss B. Kent and a Sgt. French, R.M., undertook training for its members.

Girls Training Corps

This large group photograph was taken at the council school. Recognised in the *back row* are: Angela Mullins, Pamela House, Marie White, Valerie Turpin, Kathleen Jago, Peggy Pearse, Audrey Winston, Jean Pollard, Eileen Pearse, Dorren Sandercock, Clare Hodge. *Middle row*: Joyce Tregembo, Dorothy Ford, Dorothy Spry, Miss B. Kent, Daphne Freemantle, Doreen West, Mildred Holmes, Ernistine Short, Betty Brady, Barbara Pridde, Dorothy Jones. *Front row*: Margaret Hingston, Vera Hingston, Kathleen (evacuee), Louisa Willcocks, Margaret Gilley, Eveline Willcocks, Joyce Singleton, Queenie Sargent and ? Lang.

SEARCHLIGHT BATTERIES

Enemy planes coming in to bomb Plymouth would sometimes approach the city from the east or fly over Ivybridge towards targets in Wales or the Midlands. There were two searchlight batteries operating in this area one at Lee Mill and a much larger one at Westlake on high land belonging to Mr. S. Pearse's Coyton Farm. A temporary unit was set up alongside the Exeter Road in Ivybridge but no details have been found about it apart from a remark that it had a very powerful single beam.

The Westlake battery was set up a few days before the outbreak of war with one searchlight operated by ten men some sleeping in an old double decker bus formerly used as a caravan in a nearby field. Diesel generators provide the power for this light and another two which completed the unit. By this time a small camp had been set up guarded with a fence and a machine gun and linked to a nearby ack-ack gun. Forty personnel made up the complement of staff who maintained a round the clock duty for most of the war.

During the raids on Plymouth the searchlight beams would pick up enemy aircraft and on one occasion the battery was fired upon from a plane diving low overhead. The nearby ack-ack unit would go into action when a plane was spotted. There was hutted accommodation, water had to be collected from the farmhouse and its telephone used when contacting military units elsewhere. Most of the personnel came from away although Walter Munsen spent part of his time here.

The other battery was at Hitchcombe Farm, Lee Mill, but not on so high ground. The two batteries were in contact with one another and with others at Plympton and at Noss Mayo.

Searchlight Personnel at Westlake

It is not known when this group photograph was taken but it probably records a duty shift of men with an officer and other ranks ready to keep vigilance over the Ivybridge area or about to go on a night shift hoping to pick up an enemy plane for the nearby gunners to aim at.

Remembrance Parade 1955

The war memorial is suitably decked with flowers and wreaths added to by Captain Walter S. Harvey and watched by part of the parade. Recognised are Jennifer Gilbert, Bob Elford, Frank Luckham, Ern Cox, Robin Shepherd, Brian Prettijohn and Mrs. Ryan among others.

SAVINGS CAMPAIGNS

Throughout the whole of the war years an astonishing range of savings campaigns took place in the Ivybridge area to raise money for the war effort. Thousands of pounds were raised in a great variety of ways by a great many people including school children. Such was the feeling in those days that an almost unlimited response was made to meet targets, often exceeding them when such things as tanks, planes, etc. were the object of the campaign.

There was the regular National Savings movement into which people could put their savings but this was not highlighted so much as the more exciting weekly campaigns. The extracts from local reports below give a good idea of the range of events that took place and the response made to them by all people in the area. The weekly campaigns centred on such things as *Salute the Soldier, Wings for Victory* and *Warships Week,* flag days covered *Aid to China, Aid to Russia, Red Cross Funds* and money for *Prisoners of War* sometimes directly channelled to local men known to be held in enemy hands.

There were also spontaneous activities such as street collections, selling of things made by people or children either in homes, schools or on the streets. The variety was endless and the response magnificent. It is now difficult to imagine how these events engendered such a response but the results speak for themselves. The people of Ivybridge, like those in other areas, gave of their best which was often acknowledged in the local press, by different high ranking officers coming to the presentations, such as for the adopted ship H.M.S. *Harrier* and for the various march pasts.

Local Reports

Spitfire Week was opened at Ivybridge when a lamb was auctioned at the market. The fund is in aid of the appeal for the Devon Air Squadron. A house to house collection raised £15 8s. 11d. and the children of the council school did their bit by selling scrap iron realising £2 10s. The young farmers held a dance in the *London Hotel* Assembly Room and made a gift also of £2 10s. *November 1940*

Aiming modestly at £5,000 for the summer drive of the War Savings Campaign, Ivybridge has exceeded that figure. The thermometer at the post office is rising steadily, the red indicator is leaping up rapidly. There is already a promise of a further £1,000. Good work is being done by Mr. F. Wilson, secretary of Portals Mills, while Mr. James is acting as secretary. Mr. W. Love, postman at Ivybridge who is keeping the score, said collections brought in £100 last week. Mr. O. Williams, another collector, brought in a cheque for £385. *August 1941*

Ivybridge to raise £5,000: A summer drive campaign for the purchase of a tank by the National Savings movement has started in Ivybridge. The organisers, W. S. Lane and F. Wilson, aim at raising £5,000. *August 1941*

There was a good response at Ivybridge last week to the flag day help for Aid to China week organised by Mrs. Morrice of West Park and Miss O. E. Hoarze. £15 19s. 6d. was raised through flag selling assisted by Mrs. H. Mahaer, Mrs. F. Priddle, Mrs. W. Winston, Mrs. E. Hand and Miss Alice Daniels. *March 1943*

Messrs. W. Love and F. Wilson represented Ivybridge National Savings Group, they were its main promoters. *May 1943*

Events for Salute the Soldier Week in Ivybridge are a whist drive arranged by Mrs. Lowry, dance in the Masonic Hall by the Young Farmers Club, Mrs. A. Roberts has planned a social, open air display by the A.T.C., Girls Training Corps and Army Cadets in a field lent by Messrs. Mattacott (Costly Street), a whist drive by Mrs. Williams and an open Tug-o-War competition and sports in a field in Cinder Lane. *May 1944*

Salute the Soldier! Salute him with Savings. Ask yourself this: "Am I saving to the utmost limit to back up such men as these? Can I save more... to SALUTE THE SOLDIER."

Ivybridge Plans

Ivybridge "United Aid to China Fund" committee, of which Mr. J. T. Yabsley is chairman and Mr. H. W. Blight hon. treasurer, is shortly to call a meeting, at which it is hoped every church, school, organisation and group will be represented.

"We are determined that Mme. Chiang Kai Shek's request that China should receive the friendship, fellowship, understanding and help of the British people shall find true expression in Ivybridge," says Mr. E. W. Hands hon secretary of the committee.

The date of the first representative meeting will soon be announced.

Salute the Soldier Week

Part of the march past in May, 1944, with civil defence personnel passing the saluting base. Recognised are Mrs. Helen Talbot, Sam Daniels, E. Hurrell, C. Walker, Colonel the Rev. M. S. C. Campbell, taking the salute, accompanied by an American officer and local officials.

Saving Campaigns
Prisoner of War Fund
Aid to China
Warships Week
National Saving Certificates
Penny a Week for the Red Cross
Wings for Victory Week
Salute the Soldier Week
Overseas Troops Tobacco League
Aid to Russia
Tanks for Attack Fund
British Sailors Society Fund

IVYBRIDGE
Open-air Service and March-Past

Prior to the official opening of Ivybridge "Salute the Soldier" effort, on Thursday of last week, Plympton Youth Club gave it a start with a splendid choral and dramatic entertainment, in the Methodist Schoolroom.

The church parade and combined open-air service in Victoria Park was most impressive. Besides leading the procession, the Royal Marine Band (Plymouth Division) provided music for the hymns. Accompanying the Vicar on the platform were Mrs. Phear and Mr. Parnell, representing the Methodist an' Congregational churches, respectively.

The march-past at the War Memorial was a magnificent spectacle. Col. the Rev. M. S. C. Campbell, accompanied by a representative body, took the salute. Col. Campbell, C.I.E., C.B (Military), R.A. (retired), holds the Burma 1886-7 Medal and clasp, China, 1900. He was present at the relief of Peking, being mentioned in despatches, and holds the medal and clasp. In 1912 he was awarded the Albert Medal.

As the R.M. Band reached the saluting base it swung into position to play appropriate music for the various units. Heading the parade were Royal Naval and Royal Marine contingents, and they were followed by W.R.N.S., R.A.F., R.O.C., Home Guard, Allied troops, N.F.S. (Overseas) males, N.F.S. females, A.T.C., A.R.P., Red Cross Cadets, G.T.C, Cubs and Brownies.

Social Events

On Monday, both Mrs. Hands' whist drive, at the White House, and the dance arranged by Miss P. Gillard and her Young Farmers' Committee, were successful; as was also Tuesday's social in the Masonic Hall (arranged by Mrs. A. Roberts).

Whist and bridge drives arranged by Mrs. W. Hands, on Monday and Wednesday, at the White House, resulted as follows:—
Whist—Ladies: 1, Mrs. Kelsaw; 2 Mrs. Mattacott; 3, Mr. Jemmett. Gents: 1, Mrs. Hingston; 2, Mrs Heath; 3, Miss Woodley.
Bridge.—Ladies: 1, Mrs. Tant; 2 Mrs. F. Hoare; 3, Mrs. Tickner. Gents: 1, Mrs. Fremantle; 2. Mr Baber; 3, Mrs. F. Baker. M.C. Mrs. Fremantle.

Newspaper Reports

Salute the Soldier Week
May, 1944

Youth Night

The newly-formed Youth Club acquitted themselves well on Wednesday evening (Youth night) in a number of athletic events and displays. In one of the principal races — the mile relay — Army Cadets beat A.T.C.

Red Cross Cadets (under Miss Phillips) gave a display. The Air Training Corps' "Rescue from a burning plane," was one of the high-lights, in which the lads showed considerable efficiency at fire fighting and first aid. They were trained for this display by Messrs. Brown and Keyte.

A G.T.C. parade in Costly Street was watched by hundreds of people, who were impressed at their smartness. The girls had been trained by Sgt. French R.M. and their Commandant (Miss B. and their Commandant (Miss B.

Ivybridge reached its target of £6,000 on Tuesday.

LEE MILL
Inspiring Address by Naval Officer

Following a parade and march past of the Services, N.F.S., Home Guard, and A.T.C., Lieut.-Commander F. G. Barnes, R.N., gave an inspiring address to open events at Lee Mill, on Saturday. The salute was taken by Major Masters, R.A.

Also present were Mr. Cosway, Chairman of Lee Mill Social Club; Mrs. Bassett, hon. secretary, Lee Mill Savings Group; Lieut. De Fleury, R.N.V.R., and Lieut. Wheeler, Home Guard.

Afterwards, a football match was played, in which R.N. beat N.F.S. by 3 goals to 1. A dance, in the Mission Room, followed.

On Monday, a successful concert took place in the Sunday School; and a whist drive in the Social Room on Tuesday evening.

At this early stage of the week it was announced, the target of £5,000 had been reached.

Wings for Victory Week
May 1945

IVYBRIDGE
Nearly £11,000, and a "Fair Sum" to Come

"Well done, Ivybridge!" is the message sent by Mr. W. Love, chairman of the local savings committee.

"I want to say a big 'Thank you' to all who have helped to make our Week such a success," he told a "South Devon Times" reporter. "We must remember when we hear results from the big centres, that we, per head of population, have done equally well.

"I saw practically nothing of the social side, my business being the gathering and accounting of the sheckels," Mr. Love went on.

"On Saturday there was steady business at the Post Office and Lloyds Bank. How far short of our target of £5,000 we seemed to be! But enthusiasm was soon aroused.

"Sunday morning saw the procession—pageantry indeed — followed by an impressive service in Victoria Park, greatly helped by Mr. H. W. Blight and his combined choirs, and conducted by Col. the Rev. M. S. C. Campbell, with Leading Aircraftsman Jones reading the Lesson.

"On Monday (Market Day) business was brisk, and the first £1,000 reached. On Tuesday money came in steadily; by Wednesday evening £3,700 was recorded. Thursday was a great day, and we climbed to £7,150. Friday brought us to £9,050, and, on Saturday, we had reached £10,601, with a fair sum still to come in.

£250 Free Gift

Mr. G. Perree, who has worked hard as hon. secretary of the social side of the Week, is to be congratulated on the success of his efforts.

A sum of over £250 is to be forwarded to the Chancellor of the Exchequer as a free gift.

Outstanding events, in addition to those reported last week, were the play "The Dover Road," presented by the Plympton Youth Drama Group, in the Methodist Schoolroom. It was a great success, and as a result £21 14s. 9d. was raised.

Miss Ruby Bailey was responsible for a children's dancing display on the Monday, which raised a sum of £12 15s. 6d.

Whist and Rabbits

Mrs. Lowry, of the Masonic Hall, was active during the week with three whist drives, which brought in £9 4s. 3d. Mrs. W. Hands handed over £3 from bridge and whist drives. Erme Valley Rabbit Club show was also a success, benefiting the Fund by over £7.

A Royal Marine string orchestra played in the Masonic Hall, on Friday, with a profit of over £3.

The Week was completed by a dance (arranged by Paperworkers' Union) on Saturday, at the Kings Arms Hotel, which attracted a large crowd. Also in the Kings Arms, on Thursday and Friday nights, impromptu dances were held, at which collections produced £11 16s. 0d.

Women's Institute whist drive, £1 16s. 0d.; Mrs. Roberts's Social (with sale of flowers), £9 11s. 0d.; Constitutional Club and local licensed houses also contributed.

SALVAGE CAMPAIGNS

One part of the war effort was the many salvage campaigns organised throughout the country to save materials of all kinds which could be used in making armaments, uniforms, etc. and to reduce the need for imported goods soon under serious threat from the German U boat menace.

Many appeals for saving metal, bones, paper, cloth, rubber, etc. appeared in newspapers and soon hundreds of salvage campaigns were launched in every town and village across the land. Perhaps the most obvious sign of this was the removal of iron railings from houses, public buildings, churches, parks etc.

A salvage controller was appointed in Plympton for the whole of the district taking in Ivybridge where collection points for old tyres, metal and other materials were set up in 1940 the council undertaking to collect the scrap using a trailer hinged to a normal refuse vehicle. The W.V.S., children and many adults organised collections to which the local reports below refer. Walter House remembers being asked to take charge of the scrap in the school play ground and to keep it tidy!

There were from time to time salvage weeks aimed at, for example, collecting books or paper and Ivybridge responded whole heartedly to these appeals turning out anything that could be used in the war effort.

A letter was read at Plympton R.D.C. from the headmistress of Lee Mill School requesting a contribution in respect of the scrap metal collected by the scholars, it was turned down. *June 1940*

Church Council minute book: The church railings had not been removed and had they been 25/- per ton of metal would have been paid. *April 1942*

The paper salvage campaign held recently in Ivybridge by cadets in the A.T.C. in co-operation with the National Waste Paper Recovery Association was highly successful. Weight of books in was 12 cwt. 2 qrs., paper 1 ton, 12 cwt. 2 qrs. for which was realised £10 17 6d. *November 1942*

A successful Bones Salvage Week whist drive organised by Mrs. Galliford was held at the White House, Ivybridge, and a huge sack of bones was taken away by Mrs. Talbot for the W.V.S. *October 1944*

10th July, 1941

Dear Sir,

I have been asked by the Ministry of Supply to make a very urgent appeal for your co-operation. Scrap iron and steel are very urgently required.

Old machinery, appliances and a heavier type of scrap is usually found on farms and small holdings. Such material is one of the most vital of our war needs and what we collect in this country will release shipping space for cattle foods, fertilisers and other imports needed by farmers.

Will you, therefore, lend your aid by searching your lands for any such material and collecting it at one point convenient to a main road.

Will you, therefore, lend your aid by searching your lands for all such material

If you wish to sell it it will be purchased at 25/- a ton. Alternatively if you will donate it its total value will be sent to the British Red Cross Agricultural Fund.

Yours faithfully,
Fortescue,
Lord Lieutenant of the County of Devon.

Letter sent to all Devon farmers appealing for any scrap machinery.

Save Bones.

TOO MANY ARE STILL THROWN AWAY OR BURNT.

The humble bone from the rationed joint, or the chop-bones on the plates, can play a big part in ensuring future supplies of meat, poultry, eggs, vegetables, potatoes, bread and fruit.

After the extraction of grease and glue, the residue of bones still contains nitrogen, ammonia, phosphorous, and lime. These, together with the fragments of meat and grisle which are removed before glue-extraction, combine to make a food for animals and birds which is rich in proteins. It is mixed with foods for cattle, pigs, horses, sheep and poultry.

Every ton of salvaged bones yields about a hundredweight of this meat, which is sufficient for adding to the daily rations of 150 pigs or 8,960 hens. A ton of bones also produces sufficient fertiliser for dressing 4½ acres of ground, yielding 36 tons of potatoes or wheat to make 4,500 loaves.

The smallest bone—even a splinter of bone—from meat, game or poultry, is of immense value and should be saved for salvage. The need for bones is so urgent that thousands of tons are imported annually; yet the amount still being thrown away, burnt, or buried, is three times greater than our imports. Help to reverse the situation by saving all the bones which come into your home. JULY 44

Metal Collection

Mrs. W. S. Harvey's drapers shop is being used as a collection point for scrap metal for Ivybridge's Spitfire Fund in 1941. Betty and Doris Harvey are here in front of the shop.

AMERICAN FORCES AROUND IVYBRIDGE

The largest contingent of forces based here were the Americans who arrived in the Spring of 1943 and left for the Normandy invasion at the end of May, 1944, leaving maintenance personnel at the various camps, these leaving at the end of the same year.

There were about one and a quarter million servicemen stationed throughout the west country divided into divisions of which part of the 29th Division was based in the Ivybridge area. Their main camp was at Uphill, Exeter Road, there was a gas or fuel supply depot at Wrangaton, Stowford House was used by American officers, there were troops stationed at Delamore House, Cornwood, and towards May, 1944, hundreds of personnel were drafted here in tented encampments with all the trucks and supplies ready to move into Plymouth where about 36,000 troops embarked for the invasion of France at 06.30 on 6th June, 1944, from Devon and Cornwall.

Ivybridge was designated D-Day Marshalling area L1 with 1,000 men in tents at Cornwood, 1,500 men at Delamore House and grounds in tents and 1,500 men hutted in Ivybridge. The majority of these made their way to the landing hards at Turnchapel where men and equipment was taken on landing ship tank vessels.

Such an influx of large numbers had a dramatic effect on the Ivybridge area, the local reports giving some of the various incidents that occurred including the well remembered fight in the *White Horse* Hotel.

The Construction Battalions erected the camps, first occupied by the 1st Battalion, 116th Infantry of the 29th Division. White and coloured Americans were camped separately and much to the surprise of local people relations between them were not cordial. Training exercises were undertaken on Dartmoor and many of the Ivybridge based troops took part in the various realistic exercises that occurred at Slapton in April and May, 1944.

Relationships between these troops and local people were generally very good and through dances, Christmas parties for the children in 1943, opening of homes by families to officers and men, enjoying a drink in the local hotels and public houses, going to the cinema and walking around the locality all helped in fostering these relations.

There was even a small grass air strip at David's Cross near Ivybridge with a few tents erected nearby for small Piper Cub planes to bring in important visitors, to monitor the exercises on Dartmoor and to speed up liaison work throughout the west country.

Many people remember the build up to D Day with hundreds of vehicles, piles of ammunition boxes and a hundred and one items of equipment stacked along country lanes, occupying open spaces and eventually witnessing the departure of troops in trucks for the Normandy beaches. Towards the end of May, 1944, there were about 4,000 American troops encamped in and around the Ivybridge area.

Some Local Reports

It was reported that Lt. 1st Class Leroy Milledge of "C" Company, 329 Engineers, G.S., U.S. Forces at Stowford House crashed a U.S. Army truck at Ivybridge. *September 1943*

E. Richards "C" Comp., 392 Engineers G.S. U.S. Forces, Stowford House, was court martialled at Dartington for disposing of two 5 gallon U.S. Army G.I. petrol containing 10 (U.S.) gallons of petrol. Sentenced to confinement with hard labour for six months and forfeits two thirds of his pay for six months. (Local man fined £5 for receiving this petrol). *October 1943*

A jeep driven by Pte. Harry Stone, "B" Company, 116th Infantry, A.P.O., 29th Division, Uphill Camp, Ivybridge, was involved in an accident in Ivybridge. *October 1943*

Sgt. G. Campbell, aged 31, of "C" Comp., 116th Infantry, 1st Battalion, 29th Div. U.S. Forces, Uphill Camp, reported to the Ivybridge police that a U.S. Army raincoat, U.S. Army torch, Zippo cigarette lighter and gloves were stolen from the *King's Arms* Hotel, Ivybridge. *January 1944*

1st Lt. A. S. Anderson reported to Ivybridge police that a pair of leather shoes and eight packets of U.S. cigarettes were stolen from hut 26 at Uphill, Ivybridge. *February 1944*

Pte. E. Davis (coloured) 3877 Q.M. Gas Supply, U.S. Forces reported to Ivybridge police that at 9.30 p.m. in the *White Horse* Hotel, Ivybridge, a malicious wounding took place. Offence was admitted by T/S Leroy Smith, aged 25, of Troop A, 85th Cavalry, U.S. Forces. *April 1944*

Pte. L. Franklin, Comp. "B", 116th Infantry, A.P.O., 29th Division, Uphill Camp, was sentenced to a dishonourable discharge and confinement for 5 years hard labour at a U.S. court martial for firing 16 shots into an orderly room wounding and endangering life. *April 1944*

C. Williams, aged 26, U.S. Army Military Police, "C" Comp., 795 M.P., A.P.O. 350 was riding a U.S. motorcycle to the danger of the public and failed to stop at a signal of a police constable in uniform. Dealt with by U.S. authorities. *July 1944*

A 13 ton U.S. Army wrecker vehicle towing an amphibious Duck towards Plymouth driven by Colin MacNeven of 546th Ordnance Company, A.P.O. 122, the Duck became adrift and hit Ernest Edwards of North Filham sustaining slight injuries. *July 1944*

Pte. Channie J. Hall, 1st Battalion, 116th Infantry, 5th Company, 29th Division, U.S. Forces, Uphill Camp, Ivybridge was involved in an accident while driving a U.S. truck. *October 1944*

On Wednesday last an appreciative auidence listened to some U.S. coloured soldiers who sang negro spiritual and native songs. Sgt. Stephenson who organised the event presented the solos, duets and a varied evening's programme. It was held in the Congregational Church Hall and refreshments were served by its members. *January 1945*

Ada F. Lowe, aged 20, of Kensington, London, munitions worker, was arrested for unlawfully trespassing on government property at Uphill Camp, Ivybridge. Sentenced to 3 months imprisonment. *January 1945*

A Royal Naval Ambulance, Morris 10, driven by R. Phillips, aged 25, of the 4th Rep., R.M., Uphill Camp, Ivybridge was in collision with a R.N. truck from H.M.S. *Drake* in Fore Street, Ivybridge. *August 1945*

Chow Queue
With about 1,200 troops in Ivybridge feeding and accommodation was something of a problem. Here troops queue daily for their rations or chow brought in from the States which was the envy of local people who had to do with rations.

We Three
Almost all the photographs and records about the U.S. troops in Ivybridge came from the man on the right, Henry Hausler. He kept records of what the troops did, etc. and it is from these that were sent over from America, this brief reminder is based upon. Robert Blecker stands on the left (he was later killed) and Milton Bott.

American Servicemen
This group photograph does not record the names of the men but it does give some idea about the layout of Uphill camp and the accommodation provided in nissen huts. No doubt many people will remember these huts covering open land above Exeter Road and certainly the troops walking about the area.

Swinging High

John Elford remembers being swung by Pilot Staff Sgt. Thomas K. Turner and mechanic technician Sgt. William A. Franklin on the small grass airstrip at David's Cross probably early 1944. Note the tail of a plane on the right.

Leaving Uphill Camp

A serviceman shows his pass to the camp guard before walking into Ivybridge for possible drink or to meet local friends or go to one of the many dances held in the town.

Making Friends

There were many occasions when American serviceman were welcomed by local families. Here U.S. soldier Don Brin of "D" Company, 116th Regiment, 29th Division, is with Mr. P. and Mrs. E. Blackler in their garden at 14 Fore Street sometime in 1943. It was probably on a Sunday afternoon.

David's Cross Airstrip

This small airstrip was operational in the build up of troops in 1944 for the Normandy Landings in June. John Elford is with one of the pilots of the small Piper L4 cub planes which were used for troop exercise observations and bringing in visiting senior officers and other duties.

Important Visitor

During the build up to D Day, 6th June, 1944, General Bernard Montgomery visited many camps in the south west to boost morale and identify himself with other than British Forces. Here he is on Hangar Down in May, 1944, with Colonel Cannum officer in charge of the 116th U.S. Regiment, based at Ivybridge.

Christmas Party

Hundreds of parties were arranged for thousands of children throughout Devon and Cornwall by American forces in 1943 some seen here at Ivybridge. They were entertained, given gum, candy and a hearty meal all supplied free by the troops themselves. Perhaps some people can recognise themselves in this queue at Uphill Camp.

Modbury Children

The invitation was to many children from all around Ivybridge and transport was arranged to bring them to the American huts situated overlooking Exeter Road. The Christmas parties generated a large amount of goodwill and were a great delight for children on wartime rations.

ENLISTMENTS INTO THE SERVICES

The photographs on this page show just a fraction of the hundreds of local men and women who enrolled or who were enlisted into almost every branch of the three services. The Ivybridge Forces Reception Committee presented about 600 certificates to returning personnel in 1945 which gives a good indication of the numbers who served from this area.

At the outbreak of war there were a few personnel serving in the forces and these were the first to see active service but by 1940 conscription was well under way with monthly intakes such as the twenty-three who registered in March, 1940, and the twenty-nine in August, 1940, indicating those coming up to military age. Hundreds of personnel were to find themselves entering the war fighting in almost all its theatres with many being taken prisoner and others dying at the front, in plane crashes, etc.

Reporting for conscription was either at the Ministry of Labour or police station then off to initial training, kitting out before specialised training took place in the Navy, Royal Air Force or Army. There was a constant drain of young people from Ivybridge apart from those employed in reserved occupations.

Meeting in Sicily

Gunner Ronald Barnes, Pte. Reg Vincent and Gunner Cecil Hodge unexpectedly met in Sicily in November, 1943, having landed from a troop ship from North Africa. A local photographer recorded the meeting.

IVYBRIDGE PILOT

At one time captain of Ivybridge School football team, Sgt. Leonard Thomas Roper, eldest son of Mr. & Mrs. P. Roper, 7 Zion Street, Ivybridge, has received a commission as Pilot Officer in the R.A.F.

Age 23, he was formerly in the employ of Messrs. A. J. Edwards and Son. He volunteered for service with the Royal Air Force two and a half years ago, and graduated as a navigator in South Africa.

For six months he has been an instructor.

Lance-Corporal A. Joslin, son of Mr. and Mrs. S. H. Joslin, 4 Erme Terrace, Ivybridge, and late of Crownhill, has been mentioned in dispatches for gallantry in action, while serving with the Buffs in the North African campaign. He was wounded in the hand and leg.

Twenty-one years of age, Lance-Corporal Joslin was educated at Sutton High School, later joining the staff of Barclay's Bank, where he remained until enlistment. He was also a pupil at Plymouth School of Art. He is a grandson of the late Supt. Joslin.

Stoker Charles Maddock, R.N.

Chief P/O Carlyon, telegraphist, here serving in China.

Five Brothers Serving

This must be a record for Ivybridge when in May, 1941, a local report gives Henry Bryant serving in the Royal Navy, William, Army Catering Corps, Robert, Royal Artillery, Richard in the R.A.O.B. and Jack in the R.A.S.C. Here four of them come home on the same day seen in the back garden of 38 Fore Street in 1941.

WELCOMING HOME THE TROOPS

As the end of the war drew near in 1945 many local people were looking forward to being reunited with their loved ones; for others it was a time of great sorrow as their loved ones would not be returning home, their loss was part of the price of war.

Welcome Home Funds were set up in many towns and in Ivybridge this was started in October, 1944, under Mr. M.P. Snell at the Council School. A variety of events were organised to raise money, certificates were produced and preparations were made to welcome home servicemen and service women from May, 1945, onwards. The following reports and newspaper article give details of some of these events.

At a public meeting in Ivybridge Council School under Mr. M.P.Snell a committee has been set up to plan for the welcome home for the local servicemen. G. Leigh, W. Love, J. Freeman, R. Spargo, W. Fry, A. Gray, Mesdames P. Roberts, F. Lowry, W. Thompson and Messrs. W. Manfield, G. Sandover and A. Ridge will undertake the planning. The first meeting will be held in the A.T.C. H.Q., Factory Bridge. *October 1944*

Private William O. Ridge, of Kimberley Villas, Ivybridge was liberated at Landshut, near Munich, by American 7th Army and flown to England by Canadian airmen. He was captured at Salerno on 9th September, 1943, having gone through the African campaign with the Queen's Royal Regiment. *May 1945*

Lance Corporal Frank C. Moysey came home to his wife and parents in Fore Street, Ivybridge, following service in Libya and Greece and was taken prisoner in Crete in May, 1941. He worked in prison camps in Bulgaria and Yugoslavia and was released in April of this year by the American 14th Army. He said he would not have survived without the Red Cross parcels. *May 1945*

Ivybridge Forces Reception Committee

Sgt. William Bowden

This certificate was presented to returning troops as a token of appreciation by Ivybridge people for the sacrifices they made in their service years. Sgt. Bowden was in the T.A., called up 1st September, 1939, serving as a motor mechanic in the Middle East, France and Germany. He came out of the army in 1947 having completed an extended two years service. The certificate was signed by M.P. Snell, **A.L. Gilby and** Wilfrid Love.

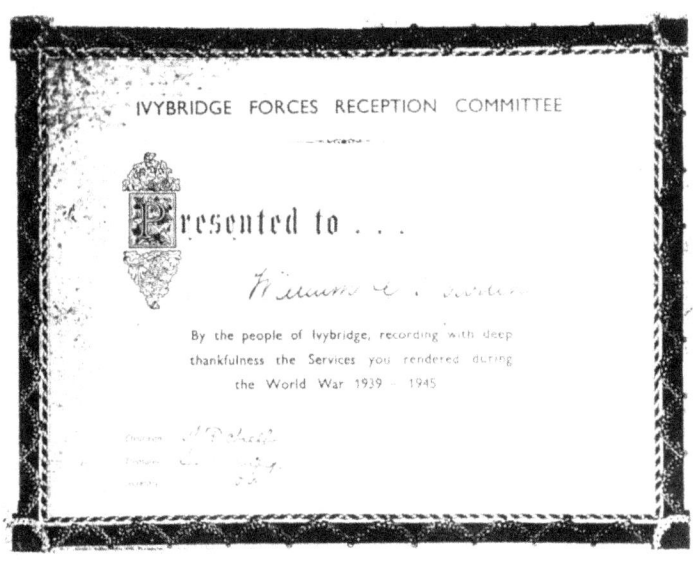

IVYBRIDGE WELCOME FOR RELEASED PRISONERS OF WAR

PTE. DOUGLAS BARNES, Queen's Royal Regt., of Bridge Park, Ivybridge, "dodged the column" when he returned on Friday after five years as a captive of the Germans and missed the public welcome that had been arranged!

Everyone was ready at the railway station to meet the down train, arriving at 9 p.m., but Pte. Barnes got off an earlier train at South Brent, "hitch-hiked" home and walked in on his surprised and delighted family.

Douglas Barnes looks fairly well but he has learned what it is to go hungry. His biggest surprise was how his brothers and sisters have grown during his five years absence. One sister has married and her wedding cake has been kept for his homecoming party.

Captured in Abbeville, in May 1940, he had some rough times but on the whole was not treated too badly. He is full of praise for the Red Cross.

A Welcome Home

Mr. W. Hands welcomes home Pte. Douglas Barnes in May, 1945, watched by W. E. Fry (Forces Reception Committee), Mr. Henry and Mrs. Bessie Barnes, Delsia and Terry, sister and brother.

SERVICE PERSONNEL STATIONED AT IVYBRIDGE

There was a surprising variety of units stationed at Ivybridge as it was considered a reasonably safe area yet not too far from Plymouth and its port. Also in the wake of the blitz on the city various government departments were transferred to the town occupying some of its larger houses. The largest influx of troops were the Americans who were camped here and undertook exercises in readiness for the Normandy Landings in June, 1944. Details of these are recorded elsewhere.

Marine W.R.E.N.S.

A contingent from Beaconville make up a section in this parade up the Fore Street for a Salute the Soldier week in 1944. P.O. Cory is leading the march and recognised are P.O. Cove, Weymouth, Parker, Goddard, Baker, Tozer, McFarlane and Withycombe.

Stowford Lodge

This was requisitioned by the Admiralty in November, 1941, and used as a cashier's office for Devonport Dockyard when it lost its own offices in the blitz. The ground floor was taken over and the cellar used for storing documents while its owners, Mr. and Mrs. J. Talbot were obliged to live in the top part of the building. Forty to fifty people worked here the majority coming out from Plymouth by lorry each day until it was released by the Admiralty in December, 1945.

Marine WRENS

Beaconville in Crescent Road was occupied by the Marine WRENS together with a nissen hut in its grounds and used as a pay and allotment office for the Royal Marines at Stonehouse Barracks, Plymouth. About sixty personnel were here under Lt. Col. E. L. N. Bishop, Paymaster. Most of the WRENS came out daily in lorries but Mary Parker, Doreen Withycombe and Barbara Morgan lived locally. Normal office hours were kept and the allotment of money from the pay of marines for their wives was undertaken here.

Air Ministry Works Department

This was a supply and maintenance depot in Costly Street serving R.A.F. stations in Devon. About twenty carpenters, electricians, painters, etc., worked from here going out by lorry to various locations undertaking maintenance work for most of the war. Materials were stored in four large buildings one of which is still standing close to the new car park. The site was guarded, it had a high perimeter fence, and entrance was given to only authorised personnel.

Royal Observer Corps

A concrete hut on Western Beacon was used for observing enemy planes from which point on a clear day much of the Devon landscape could be seen. It was manned throughout most of the war by service personnel assisted by local members of the R.O.B. In the event of low mists covering the beacon a roped walkway linked the post to the outskirts of the town.

From time to time Indian troops appeared in Ivybridge with their mules to collect clinkers from the mill furnaces. Canadian fire fighters who had come over to assist Plymouth's fire services trained at the Lee Mill camp and reports of A.T.S. in the town are recorded but their location has not been identified.

Marine WREN Barbara Carlyon in 1943
and part of her certificate of service.

PRISONERS OF WAR, RED CROSS PARCELS, ALIENS

It is a regrettable fact of war that prisoners will be taken, their families will not hear from them for months if not years and that some will die through lack of medical care or through living under very harsh conditions.

Of the dozens of local men who were called up a few were taken as prisoners. The exact number is not known but the following reports refer to three with other reports under enlistments. It brought great joy to their families and friends when they eventually returned to Ivybridge telling part of their story and hardships they endured.

William Ridge of the Queens Royal Rifles reported missing on 9th September is a prisoner of war. His parents of Belmont, Ivybridge, received a card from him saying that he is in good health, being well treated and has received his first Red Cross parcel. *November 1943*

Mrs. P. Gilbert of Mill Meadow, Ivybridge has received notification from the war office that her husband Corporal Percy Gilbert, R.A.S.C., has been killed through aerial bombardment while a prisoner of war in Germany. *September 1944*

Leading Stoker C.H. Willcocks, a survivor from H.M.S Exeter, whose wife and parents live at Mill Meadow has sent a letter home to say he has been released as a prisoner of war and is now in Australia. He was reported missing 3½ years ago and has a 4 year old son whom he has never seen. *September 1945*

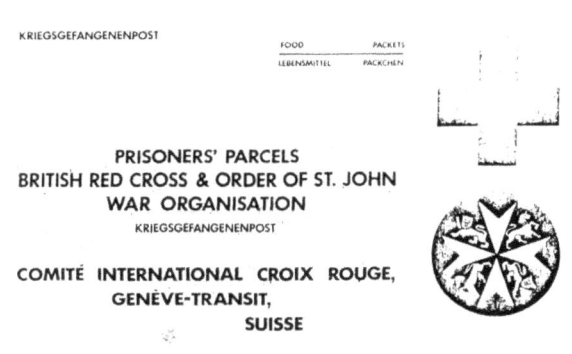

Red Cross Parcels

A large part of the Red Cross work was the despatching of food parcels to allied prisoners of war held in enemy hands. One report in 1944 says that it cost £375,000 a month to maintain this lifeline service to prisoners who, in many cases, were dependant upon receiving a parcel regularly in order that they could survive.

ALIENS RESTRICTION MOVEMENT ORDER 1940

A register of aliens was kept in the Ivybridge police station recording their names, occupations, dates of arrival and departure, particulars of any conditional employment allowed and their nationality. There were forty-three registered for the war years.

They were made up of German, Spanish, Hungarian, Belgian, American, French, Dutch, Russian, Swedish, Polish, Greek and Swiss nationalities mainly staying in this area either for a few days, weeks or in some cases longer. Some were described as being on a *temporary visit*, others as *register at once, only employment as a resident in service in a private household*. The place from which they came was also given and their destination stated when they left.

No doubt many were innocent people caught up in the war seeking refuge from Europe. However, risks could not be taken with these people which came under the general title of aliens. Some examples are given.

Oppenheim, Hans, Bullaven Hotel, musician, temporary visitor, German. August to September, 1941.
Soloneiczyk, Dora, 2 Charlton Terrace, temporary visitor, Russian. October, 1941.
Stein, Renate, N.F.S. camp, Lee Mill, fireman, Austrian. February, 1941 to May, 1944.
Gero, Lilla, The Chantry, domestic, only to enter private employment, Hungarian. January, 1940 to March, 1940.
Saez, Pedro, Cadleigh House, priest, temporary visitor, Spanish. September, 1940.

Ministry of Work camp, Uphill, Ivybridge

Towards the end of the war 163 Polish men, given as labourers, were recorded in the local register of aliens. It stated they were *Released from Polish Resettlement camps to the reserve for the purpose of employment as labourers with Plymouth Corporation on condition that they do not take any other employment without the permission of the Ministry of Employment and engage in any business without permission from the Home Office.*

They arrived at Ivybridge in 1947 having entered the U.K. in 1944 and 1945. Most of them moved into Plymouth within weeks to Manadon Camp or into private addresses.

Uphill camp was the former U.S. Army camp erected in 1943 and now partly occupied by a Ministry of Works Order for these Polish men who stayed in it for just a matter of weeks or a few months.

Devon Agricultural Executive Committee Hostel, Ivybridge

The local register of aliens records the arrival of Germans to this hostel in January, 1948, with a few directly into accommodation at Fardell Manor, Broomhill Farm, Harford, and at 7 Bridge Park. Forty-four Germans were registered with a few Polish, Ukrainian, Swiss, Yugoslav, Estonian, Rumanian and Hungarian nationalities. All were given as *farm workers* apart from a *greengrocer, cook, a domestic* and *locksmith*.

It was recorded that they had been *released from p.o.w. status for temporary work in agricultural employment*. Home Office circular dated 1947. Many were shown as leaving for Germany in 1948 and 1949.

Local farmers requested help on their land, especially at harvest, and lorries would bring out labourers and return them to the hostel on a daily basis.

SERVICE PERSONNEL WEDDINGS AT ST. JOHN'S CHURCH

These forty-one weddings give some indication of the diversity of military troops stationed around Ivybridge, their ranks, home town, etc. Many are local enrolled men married to local girls who were, in some cases, serving in the forces themselves.

James Strickland, F/O R.A.F., Exeter, to Betty Harvey, Ivybridge, August 1940
Alfred Lewden, Ldg. Stoker R.N., Plympton, to Dorothy Avery, Ivybridge, September 1940
Alexander Duncan, Pte. R.A.M.C. Stowford House, to Ivy Kingsland, Ivybridge, February 1941
Harry Richards, Seaman R.N., Plymouth, to Priscilla Thompson, Ivybridge, March 1941
John Smith, Corp. R.M., Ivybridge, to Nina MacDonald, Ivybridge, May 1941
Ernest Smale, Stoker R.N., Devonport, to Myrtle Davis, Ivybridge, June 1941
Frank Eccles, E.R. Artificer, R.N., Ivybridge, to Mavis Arnold, A.T.S. Ivybridge, June 1941
George Issac, A.B. Ldg. Seaman, Plymouth, to Gladys Hart, Ivybridge, July 1941
Frederick Goff, A.C.2 R.A.F., Ivybridge, to Lilian Davey, Ivybridge, September 1941
Philip Corker, Pte. Devonshire Reg., Cornwood, to Joan Brownless, Ivybridge, February 1942
William Davey, L.A.C. R.A.F., Ivybridge, to Patricia Salter, W.R.N.S., Ivybridge, March 1942
John Partridge, Gunner R.A., Ivybridge, to Margaret Hayes, Lee Moor, May 1942
Desmond Hill, Pte. Royal Ulster Rifles, Ivybridge, to Barbara Daniels, Ivybridge, June 1942
Kenneth Leach, A.C.2 R.A.F., Ivybridge, to Margaret Jago, Ivybridge, July 1942
William Bryant, Pte. Army Catering Corps., Ivybridge, to Kathleen Geddes, Ivybridge, July 1942
John Harvey, Sgt. Devonshire Reg., Ivybridge, to Marjorie Vivian, A.T.S., Ivybridge, July 1942
Francis Skelley, Sgt. R.A., Plympton, to Priscilla Barnes, Ivybridge, July 1942
Grenville Perkins, A.C.1 R.A.F., Modbury, to Betty Brooks, Ivybridge, August 1942
James Yabsley, F/Sgt. R.A.F., Ivybridge, to Mary Partridge, Ivybridge, August 1942
John Fiott, L/C Hampshire Reg., Ermington, to Margaret Cane, Ermington, September 1942
Arthur Terry, A.C.2 R.A.F., Bittaford, to Betty Carne, W.R.A.F., Cadeleigh Park, September 1942
Ernest Lee, L/C. R.A.S.C., Ivybridge, to Olive Tucker, Ivybridge, December 1942
Kenneth Tebbatt, L.A.C. R.A.F., Ivybridge, to Esmé Pethick, Ivybridge, February 1943
Charles Etheridge, Corp. R.M., Ivybridge, to Marjorie Avery, Ivybridge, May 1943
Frederick Brown, Yeoman of Signals, R.N., Ivybridge, to Thelma Hingston, Ivybridge, June 1943
Walter Munsen, L/Sgt. R.A., Ivybridge, to Vera Cane, Ivybridge, July 1943
William Morgan, Gunner R.A., Sheerness, to Edith Carlyon, W.R.N.S., Ivybridge, July 1943
Alexander Sturgeon, P/O R.N., Bittaford, to Crisolar Kalpakis, Bittaford, September 1943
William Pearce, P/O, R.N., Ivybridge, to Kathleen Stone, Ivybridge, December 1943
Arthur Brown, Major (Army), Oxfordshire, to Ann Rawle, A.T.S., Ivybridge, February 1944
Clarence Wakelam, L/C R.A.C., Ivybridge, to Kathleen Carne, W.A.A.F., Ivybridge, April 1944
Alfred Mullin, F/O R.A.F., Salop, to Audrey Downing, W.A.A.F., Ivybridge, August 1944
Archibald Hunter, P/O R.N., R.N. Camp Sparkwell, to Winifred Leach, Ivybridge, September 1944
John Ballard, Major, Oxford and Bucks, Oxford, to Jean Rawle, V.A.D., Ivybridge, November 1944
Arthur Groves, Driver R.A.S.C., on active service, to Marjorie White, Ivybridge, February 1945
William Barnard, E.R.A., R.N., Ivybridge, to Gladys Thorne, Ivybridge, April 1945
Victor Bill, Pte. Dorset Regiment, Lower Hansdon, Ivybridge, to Doreen Cane, Lower Hansdon, May 1945
Douglas Peacock, Lt. Army, Dagenham, to Alice Pearse, 16 Fore Street, Ivybridge, July 1945
Jessie Sutton, Pte. U.S. Army, Texas, to Jean Harper, Womens Land Army, Addicombe, Harford, July 1945
Thomas Carne, L.A.C., R.A.F., Cadleigh Park, to Nellie Hart, Womens Land Army, Cadleigh Park, October 1945
Ronald Raven, Corporal, R.A.F., Henlow, Beds., to Lillian Jeffery, M.T. Driver, Western Road, Ivybridge, December 1945

Ivybridge War Memorial
1939—1945

Booth, F. L. Sgt.	Lowden, A. R. Sto. P.O.
Broom, E. C. Sto. 1st Cl.	Northmore, G. V. F. S.Ldg. Cook
Bryant, J. Pte.	Prout, D. G. L.A.C.
Davey, A. L. Chief St.	Rogers, J. D. Pte.
Davey, C. H. Comdr.	Ryan, W. A. Surg. L/Comdr.
Frederick, J. Sto. 1st Cl.	Salter, S. C. Sto. 1st Cl.
Gilbert, P. L/Cpl.	Scantlebury, E. E. Cpl.
Gilley, W. H. Sto. P.O.	Strickland, J. M. Fl/Lt.
Harper, S. Sto. P.O.	Toms, F. Sto. P.O.
Hull, D. Rifleman	Turner, E. V. Fl/Lt.
James, D. S. A. R.N.	Yabsley, J. W/Off.
Jago, L. R. Pte.	Chadwick, S. J. Act Chief P.O.
Jarvis, E. W. Sgt.	

One Wartime Wedding

L/Sgt. Walter R. Munsen, R.A., married Vera M. Cane at St. John's Church on 3rd March, 1943, one of those recorded on this page.

VICTORY CELEBRATIONS IN 1945

By the opening months of 1945 victory in Europe was at last in sight with Allied Forces closing in on Germany along the western and eastern fronts. Hitler's reign was coming to an end. The German radio announced on 1st May, 1945, that he was dead; his forces unconditionally surrendered and VE (Victory in Europe) Day was given for 8th May. Three months later Japan surrendered and VJ (Victory over Japan) Day was declared for 14th August, 1945, so bringing to an end a terrible war in which it is estimated that about fifty-five million people died.

The whole of the United Kingdom went wild with celebrations and Ivybridge was no exception to the euphoria which swept across the land. However, for many it marked the end of a war in which family and friends had been killed or reported missing, others had been injured, some had endured the war in prison camps and soldiers, sailors and airmen were wanting to return home and to civvy street.

For the moment local people put aside their grief, there was a great air of relief and happiness that what they had put up with for almost six years had come to an end and peace looked so attractive and was welcomed with open arms.

There would still be some hardships as rationing was to go on for another nine years, many towns and cities were in ruins and the country had to face a major readjustment to peace time living.

Victory had come at last and people celebrated it in a great variety of ways at Ivybridge as these local reports recall.

IVYBRIDGE

At the time of Mr. Churchill's broadcast, at 3 p.m. on Monday, the streets of Ivybridge were absolutely deserted — everyone was indoors.

From 6.30 onwards it was the reverse, first with the crowds flocking to churches for the special services.

At the parish church of St. John, Col. the Rev. M. S. C. Campbell conducted a brief, but deeply impressive service, with Mr. H. W. Blight at the organ and the choir leading the singing of hymns appropriate to the occasion.

Congregationalists and Methodists combined for a United Service of Thanksgiving in the Methodist Church. It commenced at 6.30 with community hymn-singing, conducted by the Rev. E. D. Bonnar, led by the combined choirs under the direction of Mr. Frank Partington (organist and choirmaster). A scripture reading was given by Mr. Parnell, and the collection was for Red Cross funds.

Festivities afterwards took place both in and outdoors, in all parts of the village.

Burning Hitler

Away in the distance bonfires could be seen burning on the Beacon, Lee Moor and elsewhere. At Bridge Park, Hitler was burned in effigy. Surprising, too was the number of fireworks that had been unearthed. Was it a shopkeeper giving the public the benefit of his surplus stock on this appropriate occasion? Anyway, they were the cause of much merriment.

On Tuesday and Wednesday there were impromptu street dances from 10 p.m. until after midnight. They were arranged by Mr. and Mrs. R. E. Wright, held outside their home in Harford Road, and resulted in £7 10s. being collected for the Forces Welcome Home Fund. On Wednesday night a huge crowd congregated there and under the floodlights sang and danced until the early hours of the morning. Staff-Sergt. L. French R.M., did a fine job as M.C., and music came from radiogram and a piano acceordion played by Mr. Hughes.

Happiest Woman

The happiest woman in Ivybridge on Thursday morning was Mrs. Barnes, of Bridge Park, who had received a telegram saying that her son, Douglas, who had been a prisoner of war in German hands for several years, was in this country and would soon be home. Before the war he was employed by Mr. Bader, saddler, and his sister has since carried on in his place.

Another Ivybridge prisoner-of-war, Oliver Ridge, is safe in England.

May 1945

Message from the King

It will be seen that this is dated 1946; it was not possible to thank everyone in 1945, the task of demobbing returning troops was uppermost, the celebrations were allowed to take their course but now the King records his personal thanks to all boys and girls who played a part in the war efforts a year after peace was declared.

8th June, 1946

TO-DAY, AS WE CELEBRATE VICTORY, I send this personal message to you and all other boys and girls at school. For you have shared in the hardships and dangers of a total war and you have shared no less in the triumph of the Allied Nations.

I know you will always feel proud to belong to a country which was capable of such supreme effort; proud, too, of parents and elder brothers and sisters who by their courage, endurance and enterprise brought victory. May these qualities be yours as you grow up and join in the common effort to establish among the nations of the world unity and peace.

George R.I.

IVYBRIDGE

A special meeting of Ivybridge Parish Council was held at the Council School on Monday, August 13, when news of the impending Japanese surrender came through, and it was decided to call a public meeting on the Wednesday to organise some sort of celebrations.

The public meeting was well attended, and an open-air dance was held on the same night, and also on the following night. Children's sports were planned for Saturday, with another open-air dance in the evening. A committee was formed, comprising those members of the public who were present at the meeting. Chairman, Mr. W. Hands (chairman of Ivybridge Parish Council); secretary, Mr. Wright; treasurer, Mr. E. Taylor; with Mr. M. Coker in charge of the sports. Mrs. Percy Roberts, genr., volunteered to take charge of the teas, with a number of enthusiastic helpers. The Parish Councillors were also included in the committee.

On Saturday, in spite of the uncertain weather, a very enjoyable afternoon was spent. Music was provided by Mr. Backhouse and his amplifying equipment, and the children's races were run.

Tea was provided at the Council School, where about 250 adults were served. Some 160 children marched from the sports' field in Cinder Lane to the school. A splendid feast was given to them, complete with chocolate buns, and Mr. Hands made a short speech. One youngster confessed to have eaten 20 jam tarts, and another of having had five cups of tea!

Games were held for the children in the playground, which was being got ready for the dance to be held in the evening. Chairs were brought outside for the spectators, and additional arc lamps were set up. Crowds of people turned up to watch and take part in the dancing, and Mr. Hughes, the pianist, gave the dancers first-class music. He also played two selections on the piano-accordion. Mr. S. Cose sang two songs through the microphone and the fun went on till 11.45, Mr. R. Keay acting as pianist for part of the time. Mr. Wilfred Love then announced the end of the dance and thanked all who had helped to make the celebrations such a success. He called for three cheers for the Navy, Army and Air Force, and all who had contributed to the glorious victory and then everyone gathered round the piano to sing "There'll always be an England," "Auld Lang Syne" and "God Save The King."

During the evening collecting boxes were passed around and £5 18s. was raised for the funds of the Ivybridge Forces reception committee.

August 1945

'VICTORY TEAS' AT IVYBRIDGE

Many Parties : Nobody Left Out

Almost every child in Ivybridge must now have enjoyed a "Victory tea," there have been altogether five parties.

On June 9 about 80 children feasted in the Congregational schoolroom. They came from Bridge Park, Mill Meadow, Charlton Terrace, Exeter Road and Costly Street. Their eyes sparkled when they entered the room and saw strawberries and cream. There was a pleasant surprise later, when ice cream arrived— enough for everyone, young and old.

The guest of honour was Pte. Douglas Barnes, ex-prisoner of war.

Sports were held on the Green at Bridge Park, followed by games in the schoolroom. On leaving, each child received lemonade, home-made sweets, and a new sixpence.

The committee responsible for this successful event was Mesdames Gilbert, House, Hucker and Bastard.

The West End

On the same afternoon children of the west end also celebrated in strength, and food from almost every home was sent to Mrs. Hawkins and her body of willing helpers who provided tea for 88 in the G.T.C. Hut. Each child under three received a savings stamp for 2s. 6d., and the "overthrees" one for 6d.

Mr. W. Hillson, of Westover, gave permission for sports to be held in a field off Park Street, and after tea, the children gathered there for a full programme aranged by Mr. Coker. There were races for everyone, from under five to over forty !

At 9 p.m., the children were again taken to the Hut for supper.

Fore Street

Children of Fore Street had their feast in the Methodist Schoolroom, followed by a musical evening and games.

Those who made the arrangements are pleased at the help they received from parents and friends, which enabled them to make the "spread" a lavish one.

At Woodlands, about 20 children were entertained, on a lawn, lent by Mr. W. Dennis.

Thanks are due to Mrs. Turner and Mrs. March for the hard work they put in to ensure success of the little tea party. Everyone in the district contributed food or helped in some way.

Orthopædic Hospital

The matron of the Orthopædic Hospital has written expressing appreciation of the kindly thought which prompted the residents of Erme Terrace, Erme Road, Highland Street, Station Road, and Church Street to remember the little patients on the occasion of their Victory tea, on June 6. She enclosed two letters from the children to say "Thank You."

Celebrations in Ivybridge

These local reports make interesting reading and will probably remind many people how they joined in the various street parties, etc. some fifty years ago when the majority would have been young children.

It records that almost every child in Ivybridge enjoyed a victory tea, many maybe enjoying two, the second one being in August. Halls and huts were quickly turned into tea party rooms and with the help of many ladies and men food and entertainment were soon forthcoming.

Dances were organised, bonfires lit on the Beacon, an effigy of Hitler burnt and a dozen and more events enabled Ivybridge folk to joyously express their delight at the coming of peace.

IVYBRIDGE

Two bonfires were lit on the Beacon at Ivybridge on Wednesday night, and they could be seen for many miles around.

A dance was held in the School playground, and went on until midnight.

A public meeting was held in the Council School in the evening to arrange organised celebrations and children's sports on Saturday. A charge of 1d. on the rates will be made to cover the expenses.

V.E. Party at Woodlands

The flag decked occasion in May, 1945, shows Mrs. Churchley, Mrs. Lucy Turner, Mrs. Doris March, Mrs. Elisabeth Caseley, Mrs. Loveday Blight, Mrs. Annie Bryant, Miss Ivy Warren and Mrs. Warren. The youngsters are Shirley Burring, Anthony Churchley, Jenette Caseley, Tony Burring, Betty Burring, Cynthia Turner, Eileen Caseley, Nigel Turner, John Caseley and Sylvia Bryant, Richard Moses, Bob, Bill and Carol, Mary Hawton and Bernice Raymont.

Arthur L. Clamp – the man behind the books

Arthur Leslie Clamp was a man of boundless energy with a passion for helping others, particularly through his love of history. A printer by trade, he started his career in a printing company before moving his family from Exeter to Plymouth to teach at the Plymouth College of Art and Design, where he eventually became the Head of the Printing Department.

Arthur with his five children.

A Devoted Family Man

Despite his love of teaching, Arthur prioritised his family, always making it home by 5:30pm for tea. He and his wife, Rosemary, raised five children: Susan, Angela, Elizabeth, David, and Steven. Arthur would often combine his love of family and history by taking his children on Sunday walks, encouraging them to appreciate historical monuments by taking photos or making crayon rubbings of gravestones for his books. The family home at 203 Elburton Road was a hub of activity, with a large garden, featuring a two-storey fort and a makeshift swimming pool.

A Lifelong Learner and Adventurer

Arthur's thirst for knowledge extended beyond history to a deep curiosity about the world. He was passionate about exploring different cultures, traditions, and cuisines, often taking advantage of his long summer holidays as a teacher to travel to places like India, Russia, South America, the middle east and the USA, sometimes bringing one of his children along. This adventurous spirit even influenced his home life, as seen by the short-lived family tradition of steam-cooking vegetables after a trip to Iceland.

History is a prominent feature of family days out

Community and Philanthropic Spirit

His commitment to serving others was evident in his long-standing involvement with the Elburton Methodist Church. He was the Sunday School Superintendent for over 15 years and served as the editor of the wider church's monthly newsletter, "The Link," for a similar duration. After Rosemary's very sad passing, Arthur later remarried and, following a chance encounter with a professor from India, established a connection with a missionary school in Chennai. Together with his new wife, Christine, he co-founded a "Sponsor a Child's Education" program that continues to this day.

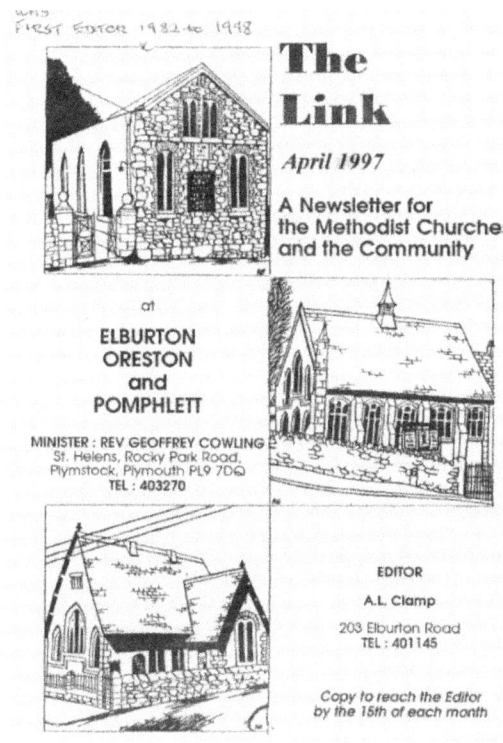

*Pictured left – The cover of 'The Link' complete
with hand drawn sketches of each church by Angela
Below right – Arthur Clamp promoting his latest book
Below left – Arthur at home with his first wife, Rosemary
Below centre – Arthur on holiday with his second wife,
Christine*

A Legacy of Learning and Positivity

Arthur's greatest passion was history, which he brought to life through tireless research, documentation, and the many books he authored. He was driven by a need to "never be stuck in a rut," constantly seeking new experiences, meeting new people, and expanding his knowledge. With a positive attitude and a great sense of humour, he was always ready to help others, leaving a lasting impact on his family and community. His children, Susan, Angela, Elizabeth, David, and Steven, remember him with love and gratitude.

David Clamp, 2025

A Legacy of Local History

Below is the story of how Arthur L Clamp began writing books, in his own words, drafted shortly before he passed away in 2001. I have only made minor alterations to this text, correcting grammatical errors that he did not survive to correct himself. When I first discovered this text, I was shocked to see my name mentioned. It seems that, unbeknownst to me, I shared my first PC with him. I suspect he used it during the day when I was at school, although I do have one memory of sitting with him and showing him how it worked. It has been a pleasure to pick up where he left off and see his books republished and redistributed, and to know that I was part of the story, even back then. It was also fascinating to discover that his pricing structure matches the way I have tried to price the books, with a third going to local sellers and the rest covering printing costs with a little left over for my expenses.

I am his eldest grandson, and it is a privilege to curate his legacy, which we are calling 'The Clamp Collection'. The very last line of the text originally reads "The following pages list all the titles." Sadly, that page is missing and we have no record of all the books he published and knowing that some of those were researched by other authors makes the process of finding them even harder. I look forward to one day completing the collection and seeing them all available again. And maybe, one day, I'll even start writing my own to add to the series. For now, here is his story in his own words.

Steven Gibson, 2025

Writing and Publishing Booklets on Local Topics and Areas

I started this interest in either 1968 or 1969 when living in Woodford. I had by these dates established the Department of Printing and I think I must have been looking for something different to do. The first titles were of A5 size proofed from type set at Clarke, Doble and Brendon, Ltd., Plymouth printers, and then made up into pages and printed at Sawtell and Neilson, Ltd., Totnes.

Then began a slow process of getting them out to shops, etc. which proved to be more time consuming and difficult than actually researching, writing and getting the books into print. However, I persisted and opened a business account with Barclays Bank on the Broadway. I was advised to give it a title so I called it "Westway Publications". There came along another problem, one of storage of paper and finished books which was solved when the family moved to Elburton in 1970.

I changed the printer to Penwell, Ltd., Callington, Cornwall, as he was then just setting up himself and his prices seemed very reasonable. I did not get any of the printers to make up the complete books. I hand folded the flat printed sheets, stitched the books on a small manual table stitcher and trimmed them in a small hand turned guillotine which I bought from someone in Penzance for £40. It was brought up in a van.

The trouble and time going to and fro to Callington was too much so I transferred the printing to PDS Printers, Prince Rock, Plymouth, and I have been with them ever since. Now they are at Plympton which is easy to reach and they fold the flat sheets which was turning out to be a long chore which only saved a small part of the printing costs.

All my first titles were written by myself. I took the photographs and developed them in the loft of the house, the type was set by now on a computer situated in the house at Elburton from which I had collected photographic lengths of text to cut up and law down as pages.

At some point I decided that I would do my own film processing of lith film so I bought a large second hand process camera from Kingsbridge and learnt through trial and error to make line negatives of the text and halftone negatives of the illustrations which proved more difficult than I anticipated. The main problem was trying to keep the developer in the large dish at the correct temperature as any change would affect the developing time. I replaced this old camera with a brand new one bought from Croydon, Surrey, costing £900. This has turned out to be a great asset cutting out an expensive part of the printer's costs and one crucial aspect of the work which I could control.

By the middle 1970s there were many outlets I had contacted in Plymouth, up to Dartmoor, Exeter, around to Torbay, Totnes, Dartmouth and the South Hams. The market for local books was much greater than I had first thought and through getting to know many local people undertaking research themselves had the chance to help and make up books for other people who had in most instances, got together a collection of photographs with some text in a rather muddled way. Through my experience in print I was able to shape up their work and get it into print and in every case I had to pay the printer and let the person have the royalties. In the majority of titles produced in this manner this was another way of producing titles and it did give some profit to my work. However, I must say that in a few cases I lost out by either the other person getting the numbers wrong, not returning any monies from stock I delivered or they thought that more of their books should have been sold.

The print run was usually 1,000 copies and from time to time I have had reprints of 250 copies. It took about ten years to clear the first print run so I always had large stocks in the garage, workshop, etc. The numbers sold during the early years was about 7,000 copies a year increasing to around 9,000 copies and for the whole of the enterprise about 500,000 have been sold. The booklets have become part of the local scene and many people collect them, shops regularly order copies and I go around certain areas month by month restocking or replacing titles as necessary.

During the past year or so I have started setting the text on a Packard Bell PC, something which I should have done some years back. I share it with Steven Gibson, my grandson. There appears to be no end to the market for local books, but I could not earn a regular income because of the long time it takes to sell stock.

However, now exceeding 100 titles made up mainly of A4 twenty-four page booklets, some folded guides, with selling prices set with a third going to the shop which is the trade custom, the original idea has been quite successful and could go on for ever.

Apart from monetary benefits, however spasmodically these might be, I have learnt a lot myself, met many interesting people and have become part of the local scene with requests to give talks and to advise people about getting into print.

Arthur L Clamp, 2001

This newspaper article, published by the Evening Herald on 17th August 2001, forms a good record of his life. Just as he encourages us to learn more about local history, we encourage you to learn a little about him. For that reason, we have included these pages at the back of all the most recently republished books, in honour of his memory and recognition of his contribution to the community.

www.ingramcontent.com/pod-product-compliance
Lightning Source LLC
Chambersburg PA
CBHW061403070526
44584CB00031B/4151